South Shore School
4800 S. Henderson St.
Seattle, WA 98118

CRITICAL ANTHOLOGIES OF NONFICTION WRITING™

CRITICAL PERSPECTIVES ON THE INDUSTRIAL REVOLUTION

Edited by
JOSH SAKOLSKY

THE ROSEN PUBLISHING GROUP, INC.
NEW YORK

To Stacy, whose patience and assistance made it possible

Published in 2005 by The Rosen Publishing Group, Inc.
29 East 21st Street, New York, NY 10010

Copyright © 2005 by The Rosen Publishing Group, Inc.

First Edition

All rights reserved. No part of this book may be reproduced in any form without permission in writing from the publisher, except by a reviewer.

Library of Congress Cataloging-in-Publication Data

Critical perspectives on the Industrial Revolution / edited by Josh Sakolsky.—1st ed.
  v. cm. — (Critical anthologies of nonfiction writing)
Includes bibliographical references and index.
Contents: Time, continuity, and change: origins of the revolution—Science, technology, and society: a changing world—People, places, and environments: faces of the revolution—Production, distribution, and consumption: impact of the revolution—Power, authority, and governance: a new world order—Culture: the legacy of the revolution—Timeline.
ISBN 1-4042-0062-2 (library binding)
1. Industrial revolution—United States—Juvenile literature.
2. Industries—United States—History—Juvenile literature.
3. Technological innovations—Social aspects—United States—History—Juvenile literature. 4. Industrialization—History—19th century—Juvenile literature. 5. Industrial revolution—Juvenile literature. [1. Industrial revolution.] I. Sakolsky, Josh. II. Series.
HC105.C88 2005
330.973'05—dc22

2003026840

Manufactured in the United States of America

On the cover: Workers at the Olympian Cotton Mills in Columbia, South Carolina, circa 1905.

CONTENTS

	Introduction	*4*
CHAPTER ONE	Time, Continuity, and Change: ORIGINS OF THE REVOLUTION	*9*
CHAPTER TWO	Science, Technology, and Society: A CHANGING WORLD	*38*
CHAPTER THREE	People, Places, and Environments: FACES OF THE REVOLUTION	*59*
CHAPTER FOUR	Production, Distribution, and Consumption: THE IMPACT OF THE REVOLUTION	*85*
CHAPTER FIVE	Power, Authority, and Governance: A NEW WORLD ORDER	*119*
CHAPTER SIX	Culture: THE LEGACY OF THE REVOLUTION	*141*
	Timeline	*164*
	For More Information	*166*
	For Further Reading	*167*
	Annotated Bibliography	*169*
	Index	*173*

INTRODUCTION

"In his classic study of modern economic history, *Industry and Empire*, the renowned economic historian Eric Hobsbawm writes, "The Industrial Revolution marks the most fundamental transformation of human life in the history of the world recorded in written document." While many historians have debated just when this chain of events started, the causes for its beginning, and who first coined the term "Industrial Revolution," Hobsbawm's analysis of its significance to world history is still valid.

Prior to the start of the Industrial Revolution during the mid-eighteenth century, developments in France and in England had led to a sort of factory system. These early "factories" were based around craftsmen doing piecework, by hand, which would then be assembled into a finished product. Prior to this, goods had been manufactured under the guild system, where production was in the hands of a master craftsman, who would work on an individual piece from start to finish, with the assistance of apprentices who were learning the craft. These new factories were more efficient. At the same time, the factories still had many of the characteristics of the guilds they had come to replace, such as a feeling of mutual obligation between the laborers and the owners. As this change in manufacturing was taking place, a "revolution" in agricultural

INTRODUCTION

practices was also peaking. These new inventions sustained England's population growth, a population that, in turn, took advantage of these technological innovations.

By the middle of the eighteenth century, new technological developments began to radically change the nature of manufacturing in England. Coal began to replace timber as the source of fuel for iron making. Since coal was abundant, easier to transport, and produced better-quality metal, demand for this new fuel skyrocketed. However, mining it at any depth was difficult because of flooding. The introduction of the Newcomen steam engine around 1710 helped drive pumps to remove the water in mines, thus permitting the exploitation of deeper and deeper coal mines. The steam engine was a huge catalyst for change as it was brought to bear on other uses.

With James Watt's version of the steam engine in 1769, steam power became more efficient and was harnessed to looms and spinning machines. This development, when combined with prior inventions such as John Kay's flying shuttle, James Hargreaves's jenny, and Samuel Crompton's mule, allowed cloth and textiles to be produced at rates and in numbers that completely overshadowed previous methods of production.

The steam engine also allowed the creation of new means of transporting these goods to ever-expanding markets, which were also needed to support the material being produced. During the 1760s, James Brindley designed England's first viable canal in Bridgewater, England, to transport coal and other raw materials to the factories. Experiments with railways, powered by animal or human energy, were also taking place at this time. The invention of steam power gave rise to many attempts to harness this new means of locomotion to the railways. In response to a contest, Englishman George Stephenson and his son developed the first successful modern steam locomotive, the Rocket, in 1829. Soon, railroads based on steam locomotives grew explosively across England. In just fifteen years, 2,441 miles (3,928 kilometers) of track had been laid to carry not only cargo but people as well. More than 30 million people rode the rails that year in England, leading to great changes in Great Britain's society and culture.

Once industrialization had taken a firm hold in England, it wasn't long before many in the United States sought to emulate the phenomenon. Nothing exemplifies this more than Samuel Slater and his creation of America's first power textile mill in Rhode Island in 1793. Slater worked in a Derbyshire, England, textile mill employing Richard Arkwright's machinery, which was the basis for the first large-scale textile factories, though it used water, not steam, as its primary source of power. Slater immigrated to the United States at the age of twenty-one. He quickly settled in Pawtuckett, Rhode Island, and with the help of financial backers re-created and adapted Arkwright's technology from memory to create America's first successful textile factory.

Soon, the United States would take advantage of the other technological advances coming out of England, and by 1830, America's first railways had become operational. For a country of much larger proportions than England, this new technology would help link the lines of western settlement with the growing industrial centers on the northeastern seaboard. After 1848, Chicago became the main hub for transportation, with many different rail lines and a canal system terminating there. This would be the city's greatest asset and one of the reasons it would become the nation's center of commodity trading.

After the Civil War (1861–1865), the pace of industrialization continued to accelerate rapidly. Throughout the 1870s and 1880s, American manufacturers adopted new technological improvements in steel production that let them slowly overtake Great Britain's dominance in this market. As more and more people moved to America's cities to take advantage of all these opportunities, the character of the United States changed. America was no longer a land dominated by farmers, but one dominated by city dwellers living off of wages. This would lead to periodic outbreaks of strong labor unrest as workers attempted to gain a larger share of the wealth that they were instrumental in producing.

During the same period, many of these workers were newly arrived immigrants whose understanding of America's culture and language was usually poor. This led to considerable tension in urban communities. Starting in the 1880s and not fully ending until the 1920s, great waves of immigrants from southern and eastern Europe landed on America's shores, settled in its cities, and sought to find work in its factories. As industrialization also continued to gather greater force in the North, many African Americans started to move there after Reconstruction's end. This great migration, which would eventually end in the 1940s, also brought America's inherent racism to the forefront as many of these "internal immigrants" found that the prejudice they tried to escape in the South was just as entrenched in the North.

These were just some of the transformations that industrialization wrought as its effects spread across the United States and eventually the world. The selections included in this volume represent a few of the ideas and experiences that various groups had throughout their encounters with this overwhelming force for change. They have been organized in a thematic fashion to fully demonstrate how deeply the Industrial Revolution reached all aspects of Americans' lives. This book, however, is not intended to convey the definitive "story" of the Industrial Revolution. Instead, these pieces are a doorway to an event that irrevocably shaped the United States and the world, and whose effects and consequences are felt to this day.

CHAPTER ONE

TIME, CONTINUITY, AND CHANGE: ORIGINS OF THE REVOLUTION

"The Nineteenth Century"
From The Outline of History
By H. G. Wells
1949

As one of the first writers to popularize the science fiction novel, Englishman H. G. Wells gained fame with such books as The Time Machine, The Invisible Man, The War of the Worlds *and* The Island of Dr. Moreau. *His popularity stemmed from the way in which he was able to fully envision the consequences of the technologies that were encroaching on modern life.*

Some of this ability was developed through his training in science and his work as a science teacher. He had studied under the famous biologist and proponent of Darwinism, T. H. Huxley, and he had a firm grasp of the biological implications of evolution, including the fact that there was no guarantee that the human race itself would not become extinct. This knowledge influenced his reading of history and his political beliefs. As the following excerpt from his Outline of History *shows, Wells believed that the fate of humankind would lie not in the political developments in the nineteenth century. Instead, Wells believed it was the scientific progress inherent in the Industrial Revolution that allowed technological improvements to bring about greater economic prosperity to millions of people.*

The career and personality of Napoleon I bulks disproportionately in the nineteenth-century histories. He was of little significance to the broad onward movement of human affairs; he was an interruption, a reminder of latent evils, a thing like the bacterium of some pestilence. Even regarded as a pestilence, he was not of supreme rank; he killed far fewer people than the influenza epidemic of 1918, and produced less political and social disruption than the plague of Justinian.

The real makers of history in the nineteenth century, the people whose consequences will be determining human life a century ahead, were those who advanced and contributed to this fivefold constructive effort. Compared to them, the foreign ministers and "statesmen" and politicians of this period were no more than a number of troublesome and occasionally incendiary schoolboys—and a few metal thieves—playing about and doing transitory mischief amidst the accumulating materials upon the site of a great building whose nature they do not understand.

And while throughout the nineteenth century the mind of Western civilization, which the Renascence [Renaissance] had released, gathered itself to the task of creative social and political reconstruction that still lies before it, there swept across the world a wave of universal change in human power and the material conditions of life that the first scientific efforts of that liberated mind had made possible. The prophecies of Roger Bacon began to live in reality. The accumulating knowledge and confidence of the little succession of men who had been carrying on the development of science, now began to bear fruit that common men could understand. The first steam-engines in the eighteenth century were pumping engines used to keep water out of the newly opened coal mines. These coal mines were being worked to supply coke for iron-smelting, for which wood-charcoal had previously been employed. It was James Watt, a mathematical instrument maker of Glasgow, [Scotland,] who improved this steam pumping-engine and made it available for the driving of machinery. The first engine so employed was installed in a cotton mill in Nottingham in 1785.

In 1804 [Richard] Trevithick adapted the Watt engine to transport, and made the first locomotive. In 1825 the first railway, between Stockton and Darlington, was opened for traffic. The original engine (Locomotion No. 1, 1825) still adorns Darlington platform. By the middle of the century a network of railways had spread all over Europe.

Here was a sudden change in what had long been a fixed condition of human life, the maximum rate of land transport. After the Russian disaster, Napoleon travelled from near Vilna to Paris in 312 hours. This was a journey of about 1,400 miles. He was travelling with every conceivable advantage, and he averaged under five miles an hour. An ordinary traveller could not have done this distance in twice the time. These were about the same maximum rates of travel as held good between Rome and Gaul in the first century AD, or between Sardis and Susa in the fourth century BC.

Then suddenly came a tremendous change. The railways reduced this journey for any ordinary traveller to less than forty-eight hours. That is to say, they reduced the chief European distances to about a tenth of what they had been. They made it possible to carry out administrative work in areas ten times as great as any that had hitherto been workable under one administration. The full significance of that possibility in Europe still remains to be realized. Europe is still netted in boundaries drawn in the horse and road era. In America the effects were immediate. To the United States of America, sprawling westward, it meant the possibility of a continuous access to Washington, however far the frontier travelled across the continent. It meant unity, sustained on a scale that would otherwise have been impossible.

Concurrently with the development of steam transport upon land and sea a new and striking addition to the facilities of human intercourse arose out of the investigations of [Alessandro] Volta, [Luigi] Galvani, and [Michael] Faraday into various electrical phenomena. The electric telegraph came into existence in 1835. The first underseas cable was laid in 1851 between France and England. In a few years the telegraph system had spread over the civilized world, and news which had hitherto travelled slowly from point to point became practically simultaneous throughout the earth.

These things, the steam railway and the electric telegraph, were to the popular imagination of the middle nineteenth century the most striking and revolutionary of inventions, but they were only the most conspicuous and clumsy first fruits of a far more extensive process. Technical knowledge and skill were developing with an extraordinary rapidity, and to an extraordinary extent, measured by the progress of any previous age.

Far less conspicuous at first in everyday life, but finally far more important, was the extension of man's power over various structural materials. Before the middle of the eighteenth century iron was reduced from its ores by means of wood-charcoal, was handled in small pieces, and hammered and wrought into shape. It was material for a craftsman. Quality and treatment were enormously dependent upon the experience and sagacity of the individual ironworker. The largest masses of iron that could be dealt with under those conditions amounted at most (in the sixteenth century) to two or three tons. (There was a very definite upward limit, therefore, to the size of cannon.) The blast furnace arose in the eighteenth century, and developed with the use of coke. Not before the eighteenth century do we find rolled sheet iron (1728) and rolled rods and bars (1783). [James] Nasmyth's steam hammer came as late as 1839.

Parallel with this extension of mechanical possibilities the new science of electricity grew up. It was only in the eighties of the nineteenth century that this body of inquiry began to yield results to impress the vulgar mind. Then suddenly came electric light and electric traction; and the transmutation of forces, the possibility of sending power, that could be changed into mechanical motion or light or heat as one chose, along a copper wire, as water is sent along a pipe, began to come through to the idea of ordinary people . . .

The mechanical revolution itself began, we may say, with the exhaustion of the wood supply for the ironworks of England. This led to the use of coal, the coal mine led to the simple pumping-engine, the development of the pumping-engine by Watt into a machine-driving engine led on to the locomotive and the steamship. This was the first phase of a great expansion in the use of steam. A second phase in the mechanical revolution began with the application of electrical science to practical problems and the development of electric lighting, power-transmission, and traction.

A third phase is to be distinguished when, in the eighties, a new type of engine came into use, an engine in which the expansive force of an explosive mixture replaced the expansive force of steam. The light, highly efficient engines that were thus made possible were applied to the automobile, and developed at last to reach such a pitch of lightness and efficiency as to render flight—long known to be possible—a practical achievement.

The work of the Wright brothers in America was of primary importance in this field. A flying-machine—but not a machine large enough to take up a human body—was made by Professor [Samuel P.] Langley, of the Smithsonian Institution of Washington, as early as 1897. His next effort, a full-size aeroplane, failed on its early trials, but after very extensive alterations was successfully flown by [Glenn H.] Curtiss a few years later. By 1909 the aeroplane was available for human locomotion.

There is a tendency in many histories to confuse together what we have here called the *mechanical revolution*, which was an entirely new thing in human experience arising out of the development of organized science, a new step like the invention of agriculture or the discovery of metals, with something else, quite different in its origins, something for which there was already an historical precedent, the social and financial development which is called the *industrial revolution*.

The two processes were going on together, they were constantly reacting upon each other, but they were in root and essence different. There would have been an industrial revolution of sorts if there had been no coal, no steam, no machinery; but in that case it would probably have followed far more closely upon the lines of the social and financial developments of the later years of the Roman Republic. It would have repeated the story of dispossessed free cultivators, gang labour, great estates, great financial fortunes, and a socially destructive financial process.

The mechanical revolution, the process of mechanical invention and discovery, was a new thing in human experience, and it went on regardless of the social, political, economic, and industrial consequences it might produce. The industrial revolution, on the other hand, like most other human affairs, was and is more and more profoundly changed and deflected by the constant variation in human conditions caused by the mechanical revolution. And the essential difference between the amassing of riches, the extinction of small farmers and small business men, and the phase of big finance in the latter centuries of the Roman Republic on the one hand, and the very similar concentration of capital in the eighteenth and nineteenth centuries on the other, lies in the profound difference in the character of labour that the mechanical revolution was bringing about.

The power of the Old World was human power; everything depended ultimately upon the driving power of human muscle, the muscle of ignorant and subjugated men. A little animal muscle, supplied by draft oxen, horse traction, and the like, contributed. Where a weight had to be lifted, men lifted it; where a rock had to be quarried, men chipped it out; where a field had to be ploughed, men and oxen ploughed it; the Roman equivalent of the steamship was the galley with its banks of sweating rowers.

To trace any broad outlines in the fermentation of ideas that went on during the mechanical and industrial revolution of the nineteenth century is a very difficult task. But we must attempt it if we are to link what has gone before in this history with the condition of our world to-day.

Excerpt from The Communist Manifesto
By Karl Marx
1848

Karl Marx published his Communist Manifesto *pamphlet in January 1848, and the ideas in it would become some of the most influential and debated during the next 150 years. Believing that the course of history was shaped by economic forces and the groups that controlled them, Marx sought to create a society that gave workers a controlling share in the means of production. With the financial support of his partner and patron, Friedrich Engels, Marx continued to publish works that would move and inspire workers and intellectuals to band together to try and implement his vision of a utopian society where those who worked would not want for material goods. Marx's work heavily criticized the bourgeoisie (the middle class) while rallying support for the proletariat (the working class). Marx's ideas would influence Vladimir Lenin, who would use them as a rallying cry during the Russian Revolution to overthrow the czar near the end of World War I (1914–1918). Lenin and his Bolshevik Party would defeat the Mensheviks, a rival revolutionary group, and then go on to establish the Communist Soviet Union. This was a state based on Marx's Communist ideas as modified by Lenin. However, the Soviet Union never provided the freedoms and economic security for its people that Marx propounded. In 1989, the Soviet Union collapsed under the weight of its own economic inefficiencies and lack of political freedoms, leaving behind a legacy not of freedom from want but a trail of terror and repression instead.*

The weapons with which the bourgeoisie felled feudalism to the ground are now turned against the bourgeoisie itself.

But not only has the bourgeoisie forged the weapons that bring death to itself; it has also called into existence the men who are to wield those weapons—the modern working class—the proletarians.

In proportion as the bourgeoisie, i.e., capital, is developed, in the same proportion is the proletariat, the modern working class, developed—a class of laborers, who live only so long as they find work, and who find work only so long as their labor increases capital. These laborers, who must sell themselves piecemeal, are a commodity, like every other article of commerce, and are consequently exposed to all the vicissitudes of competition, to all the fluctuations of the market.

Owing to the extensive use of machinery, and to the division of labor, the work of the proletarians has lost all individual character, and, consequently, all charm for the workman. He becomes an appendage of the machine, and it is only the most simple, most monotonous, and most easily acquired knack, that is required of him. Hence, the cost of production of a workman is restricted, almost entirely, to the means of subsistence that he requires for maintenance, and for the propagation of his race. But the price of a commodity, and therefore also of labor, is equal to its cost of production. In proportion, therefore, as the repulsiveness of the work increases, the wage decreases. What is more, in proportion as the use of machinery and division of labor increases, in the same proportion the burden of toil also increases, whether by prolongation of the working hours, by the increase of the work exacted in a given time, or by increased speed of machinery, etc.

Modern Industry has converted the little workshop of the patriarchal master into the great factory of the industrial capitalist. Masses of laborers, crowded into the factory, are organized like soldiers. As privates of the industrial army, they are placed under the command of a perfect hierarchy of officers and sergeants. Not only are they slaves of the bourgeois class, and of the bourgeois state; they are daily and hourly enslaved by the machine, by the overlooker, and, above all, in the individual bourgeois manufacturer himself. The more openly this despotism proclaims gain to be its end and aim, the more petty, the more hateful and the more embittering it is.

The less the skill and exertion of strength implied in manual labor, in other words, the more modern industry becomes developed, the more is the labor of men superseded by that of women. Differences of age and sex have no longer any distinctive social validity for the working class. All are instruments of labor, more or less expensive to use, according to their age and sex.

No sooner is the exploitation of the laborer by the manufacturer, so far at an end, that he receives his wages in cash, than he is set upon by the other portion of the bourgeoisie, the landlord, the shopkeeper, the pawnbroker, etc.

The lower strata of the middle class—the small tradespeople, shopkeepers, and retired tradesmen generally, the handicraftsmen and peasants—all these sink gradually into the proletariat, partly because their diminutive capital does not suffice for the scale on which Modern Industry is carried on, and is swamped in the competition with the large capitalists, partly because their specialized skill is rendered worthless by new methods of production. Thus, the proletariat is recruited from all classes of the population.

The proletariat goes through various stages of development. With its birth begins its struggle with the bourgeoisie. At first, the contest is carried on by individual laborers, then by the work of people of a factory, then by the operative of one trade, in one locality, against the individual bourgeois who directly exploits them. They direct their attacks not against the bourgeois condition of production, but against the instruments of production themselves; they destroy imported wares that compete with their labor, they smash to pieces machinery, they set factories ablaze, they seek to restore by force the vanished status of the workman of the Middle Ages.

At this stage, the laborers still form an incoherent mass scattered over the whole country, and broken up by their mutual competition. If anywhere they unite to form more compact bodies, this is not yet the consequence of their own active union, but of the union of the bourgeoisie, which class, in order to attain its own political ends, is compelled to set the whole proletariat in motion, and is moreover yet, for a time, able to do so. At this stage, therefore, the proletarians do not fight their enemies, but the enemies of their enemies, the remnants of absolute monarchy, the landowners, the non-industrial bourgeois, the petty bourgeois. Thus, the whole historical movement is concentrated in the hands of the bourgeoisie; every victory so obtained is a victory for the bourgeoisie.

But with the development of industry, the proletariat not only increases in number; it becomes concentrated in greater masses, its strength grows, and it feels that strength more. The various interests and conditions of life within the ranks of the proletariat are more and more equalized, in proportion as machinery obliterates all distinctions of labor, and nearly everywhere reduces wages to the same low level. The growing competition among the bourgeois, and the resulting commercial crises, make the wages of the workers ever more fluctuating. The increasing improvement of machinery, ever more rapidly developing, makes their livelihood more and more precarious; the collisions between individual workmen and individual bourgeois take more and more the character of collisions between two classes. Thereupon, the workers begin to form combinations (trade unions) against the bourgeois; they club together in order to keep up the rate of wages; they found permanent associations in order to make provision beforehand for these occasional revolts. Here and there, the contest breaks out into riots.

Now and then the workers are victorious, but only for a time. The real fruit of their battles lie not in the immediate result, but in the ever expanding union of the workers. This union is helped on by the improved means of communication that are created by Modern Industry, and that place the workers of different localities in contact with one another. It was just this contact that was needed to centralize the numerous local struggles, all of the same character, into one national struggle between classes. But every class struggle is a political struggle. And that union, to attain which the burghers of the Middle Ages, with their miserable highways, required centuries, the modern proletarian, thanks to railways, achieve in a few years.

This organization of the proletarians into a class, and, consequently, into a political party, is continually being upset again by the competition between the workers themselves. But it ever rises up again, stronger, firmer, mightier. It compels legislative recognition of particular interests of the workers, by taking advantage of the divisions among the bourgeoisie itself. Thus, the Ten-Hours Bill in England was carried.

Altogether, collisions between the classes of the old society further in many ways the course of development of the proletariat. The bourgeoisie finds itself involved in a constant battle. At first with the aristocracy; later on, with those portions of the bourgeoisie itself, whose interests have become antagonistic to the progress of industry; at all time with the bourgeoisie of foreign countries. In all these battles, it sees itself compelled to appeal to the proletariat, to ask for help, and thus to drag it into the political arena. The bourgeoisie itself, therefore, supplies the proletariat with its own elements of political and general education, in other words, it furnishes the proletariat with weapons for fighting the bourgeoisie.

Further, as we have already seen, entire sections of the ruling class are, by the advance of industry, precipitated into the proletariat, or are at least threatened in their conditions of existence. These also supply the proletariat with fresh elements of enlightenment and progress.

Finally, in times when the class struggle nears the decisive hour, the progress of dissolution going on within the ruling class, in fact within the whole range of old society, assumes such a violent, glaring character, that a small section of the ruling class cuts itself adrift, and joins the revolutionary class, the class that holds the future in its hands. Just as, therefore, at an earlier period, a section of the nobility went over to the bourgeoisie, so now a portion of the bourgeoisie goes over to the proletariat, and in particular, a portion of the bourgeois ideologists, who have raised themselves to the level of comprehending theoretically the historical movement as a whole.

Of all the classes that stand face to face with the bourgeoisie today, the proletariat alone is a genuinely revolutionary class. The other classes decay and finally disappear in the face of Modern Industry; the proletariat is its special and essential product.

The lower middle class, the small manufacturer, the shopkeeper, the artisan, the peasant, all these fight against the bourgeoisie, to save from extinction their existence as fractions of the middle class. They are therefore not revolutionary, but conservative. Nay, more, they are reactionary, for they try to roll back the wheel of history. If, by chance, they are revolutionary, they are only so in view of their impending transfer into the proletariat; they thus defend not their present, but their future interests; they desert their own standpoint to place themselves at that of the proletariat.

The "dangerous class," the social scum, that passively rotting mass thrown off by the lowest layers of the old society, may, here and there, be swept into the movement by a proletarian revolution; its conditions of life, however, prepare it far more for the part of a bribed tool of reactionary intrigue.

In the condition of the proletariat, those of old society at large are already virtually swamped. The proletarian is without property; his relation to his wife and children has no longer anything in common with the bourgeois family relations; modern industry labor, modern subjection to capital, the same in England as in France, in America as in Germany, has stripped him of every trace of national character. Law, morality, religion, are to him so many bourgeois prejudices, behind which lurk in ambush just as many bourgeois interests.

All the preceding classes that got the upper hand sought to fortify their already acquired status by subjecting society at large to their conditions of appropriation. The proletarians cannot become masters of the productive forces of society, except by abolishing their own previous mode of appropriation, and thereby also every other previous mode of appropriation. They have nothing of their own to secure and to fortify; their mission is to destroy all previous securities for, and insurances of, individual property.

All previous historical movements were movements of minorities, or in the interest of minorities. The proletarian movement is the self-conscious, independent movement of the immense majority, in the interest of the immense majority. The proletariat, the lowest stratum of our present society, cannot stir, cannot raise itself up, without the whole super incumbent strata of official society being sprung into the air.

Though not in substance, yet in form, the struggle of the proletariat with the bourgeoisie is at first a national struggle. The proletariat of each country must, of course, first of all settle matters with its own bourgeoisie.

In depicting the most general phases of the development of the proletariat, we traced the more or less veiled civil war, raging within existing society, up to the point where that war breaks out into open revolution, and where the violent overthrow of the bourgeoisie lays the foundation for the sway of the proletariat.

Hitherto, every form of society has been based, as we have already seen, on the antagonism of oppressing and oppressed classes. But in order to oppress a class, certain conditions must be assured to it under which it can, at least, continue its slavish existence. The serf, in the period of serfdom, raised himself to membership in the commune, just as the petty bourgeois, under the yoke of the feudal absolutism, managed to develop into a bourgeois. The modern laborer, on the contrary, instead of rising with the process of industry, sinks deeper and deeper below the conditions of existence of his own class. He becomes a pauper, and pauperism develops more rapidly than population and wealth. And here it becomes evident that the bourgeoisie is unfit any longer to be the ruling class in society, and to impose its conditions of existence upon society as an overriding law. It is unfit to rule because it is incompetent to assure an existence to its slave within his slavery, because it cannot help letting him sink into such a state, that it has to feed him, instead of being fed by him. Society can no longer live under this bourgeoisie, in other words, its existence is no longer compatible with society.

The essential conditions for the existence and for the sway of the bourgeois class is the formation and augmentation of capital; the condition for capital is wage labor. Wage labor rests exclusively on competition between the laborers. The advance of industry, whose involuntary promoter is the bourgeoisie, replaces the isolation of the laborers, due to competition, by the revolutionary combination, due to association. The development of Modern Industry, therefore, cuts from under its feet the very foundation on which the bourgeoisie produces and appropriates products. What the bourgeoisie therefore produces, above all, are its own grave-diggers. Its fall and the victory of the proletariat are equally inevitable.

"What Is Free Trade?"
By William Graham Sumner
1934

One of the counterarguments to communism was laissez-faire capitalism, or the doctrine of limiting governmental interference in business practice. The proponents of this economic system believed that a marketplace should contain as little regulation as possible. This belief stemmed from the pioneering economist Adam Smith's dictum that the marketplace had its own self-correcting "invisible hand" that would prevent excesses of prices from weighing down consumers and keep capital from over-exploiting labor.

Free trade, or the idea that all nations should be able to trade with each other with little or no tariffs and taxes to keep each other's imports out, was an outgrowth of the laissez-faire economic theory. By increasing trade between nations and the succeeding wealth that resulted, it was thought that all members of society would eventually benefit as people were able to find new jobs in manufacturing to serve the needs of export markets. These people would also benefit as consumers because goods and commodities from other countries that could be produced cheaper than those at home would be available to them at cheaper prices. One of America's leading sociologists and political economists, William Graham Sumner, advocated extreme laissez-faire and the idea that trade would grow quickly and correct itself.

The doctrines of free trade and laissez-faire would act in opposition to Karl Marx's ideas on Communism, as groups and intellectuals throughout the nineteenth and early twentieth centuries tried to adjust to all the social and economic changes that the Industrial Revolution brought with it.

———◻———

There never would have been any such thing to fight for as free speech, free press, free worship, or free soil, if nobody had ever put restraints on men in those matters. We never should have heard of free trade, if no restrictions had ever been put on trade. If there had been any restrictions on the intercourse between the states of this Union, we should have heard of ceaseless agitation to get those restrictions removed. Since there are no restrictions allowed under the Constitution, we do not realize the fact that we are enjoying the blessings of complete liberty, where, if wise counsels had not prevailed at a critical moment, we should now have had a great mass of traditional and deep-rooted interferences to encounter.

Our intercourse with foreign nations, however, has been interfered with, because it is a fact that, by such interference, some of us can win advantages over others. The power of Congress to levy taxes is employed to lay duties on imports, not in order to secure a revenue from imports, but to prevent imports—in which case, of course, no revenue will be obtained. The effect which is aimed at, and which is attained by this device, is that the American consumer, when he wants to satisfy his needs, has to go to an American producer of the thing he wants, and has to give to him a price for the product which is greater than that which some foreigner would have charged. The object of this device, as stated on the best protectionist authority, is: "To effect the diversion of a part of the labor and capital of the people out of the channels in which it would run otherwise, into channels favored or created by law." This description is strictly correct, and from it the reader will see that protection has nothing to do with any foreigner whatever. It is purely a question of domestic policy. It is only a question whether we shall, by taxing each other, drive the industry of this country into an arbitrary and artificial development, or whether we shall allow one another to employ each his capital and labor in his own way. Note that there is for us all the same labor, capital, soil, national character, climate, etc.,—that is, that all the conditions of production remain unaltered. The only change which is operated is a wrenching of labor and capital out of the lines on which they would act under the impulse of individual enterprise, energy, and interest, and their impulsion in another direction selected by the legislator. Plainly, all the import duty can do is to close the door, shutting the foreigner out and the Americans in. Then, when an American needs iron, coal, copper, woolens, cottons, or anything else in the shape of manufactured commodities, the operation begins. He has to buy in a market which is either wholly or partially monopolized. The whole object of shutting him in is to take advantage of this situation to make him give more of his products for a given amount of the protected articles, than he need have given for the same things in the world's market. Under this system a part of our product is diverted from the satisfaction of our needs, and is spent to hire some of our fellow-citizens to go out of an employment which would pay under the world's competition, into one which will not pay under the world's competition. We, therefore, do with less clothes, furniture, tools, crockery, glassware, bed and table linen, books, etc., and the satisfaction we have for this sacrifice is knowing that some of our neighbors are carrying on business which according to their statement does not pay, and that we are paying their losses and hiring them to keep on.

Free trade is a revolt against this device. It is not a revolt against import duties or indirect taxes as a means of raising revenue. It has nothing to say about that, one way or the other. It begins to protest and agitate just as soon as any tax begins to act protectively, and it denounces any tax which one citizen levies on another. The protectionists have a long string of notions and doctrines which they put forward to try to prove that their device is not a contrivance by which they can make their fellow-citizens contribute to their support, but is a device for increasing the national wealth and power. These allegations must be examined by economists, or other persons who are properly trained to test their correctness, in fact and logic. It is enough here to say, over a responsible signature, that no such allegation has ever been made which would bear examination. On the contrary, all such assertions have the character of apologies or special pleas to divert attention from the one plain fact that the advocates of a protective tariff have a direct pecuniary interest in it, and that they have secured it, and now maintain it, for that reason and no other. The rest is all afterthought and excuse. If any gain could possibly come to the country through the gains of the beneficiaries of the tariff, obviously the country must incur at least an equal loss through the losses of that part of the people who pay what the protected win. If a country could win anything that way, it would be like a man lifting himself by his boot straps.

The protectionists, in advocating their system, always spend a great deal of effort and eloquence on appeals to patriotism, and to international jealousies. These are all entirely aside from the point. The protective system is a domestic system, for domestic purposes, and it is sought by domestic means. The one who pays, and the one who gets, are both Americans. The victim and the beneficiary are amongst ourselves. It is just as unpatriotic to oppress one American as it is patriotic to favor another. If we make one American pay taxes to another American, it will neither vex nor please any foreign nation.

The protectionists speak of trade with the contempt of feudal nobles, but on examination it appears that they have something to sell, and that they mean to denounce trade with their rivals. They denounce cheapness, and it appears that they do so because they want to sell dear. When they buy, they buy as cheaply as they can. They say that they want to raise wages, but they never pay anything but the lowest market rate. They denounce selfishness, while pursuing a scheme for their own selfish aggrandizement, and they bewail the dominion of self-interest over men who want to enjoy their own earnings, and object to surrendering the same to them. They attribute to government, or to "the state," the power and right to decide what industrial enterprises each of us shall subscribe to support.

Free trade means antagonism to this whole policy and theory at every point. The free trader regards it as all false, meretricious, and delusive. He considers it an invasion of private rights. In the best case, if all that the protectionist claims were true, he would be taking it upon himself to decide how his neighbor should spend his earnings, and—more than that—that his neighbor shall spend his earnings for the advantage of the men who make the decision. This is plainly immoral and corrupting; nothing could be more so. The free trader also denies that the government either can, or ought to regulate the way in which a man shall employ his earnings. He sees that the government is nothing but a clique of the parties in interest. It is a few men who have control of the civic organization. If they were called upon to regulate business, they would need a wisdom which they have not. They do not do this. They only turn the "channels" to the advantage of themselves and their friends. This corrupts the institutions of government and continues under our system all the old abuses by which the men who could get control of the governmental machinery have used it to aggrandize themselves at the expense of others. The free trader holds that the people will employ their labor and capital to the best advantage when each man employs his own in his own way, according to the maxim that "A fool is wiser in his own house than a sage in another man's house"; —how much more, then, shall he be wiser than a politician? And he holds, further, that by the nature of the case, if any governmental coercion is necessary to drive industry in a direction in which it would not otherwise go, such coercion must be mischievous.

    The free trader further holds that protection is all a mistake and delusion to those who think that they win by it, in that it lessens their self-reliance and energy and exposes their business to vicissitudes which, not being incident to a natural order of things, cannot be foreseen and guarded against by business skill; also that it throws the business into a condition in which it is exposed to a series of heats and chills, and finally, unless a new stimulus is applied, reduced to a state of dull decay. They therefore hold that even the protected would be far better off without it.

"Science, Invention, Industry"
By C. D. Wright
1891

At the turn of the twentieth century, the pace of technological change and industrialization was rapidly accelerating. During the height of the Industrial Revolution, cultural commentators noted that the United States was becoming an industrial and economic world power. Essays and books came pouring out, explaining which unique features of American society had made this force of progress happen. While highlighting all of the benefits that these new technologies brought, many of these articles failed to note the costs of rapid industrialization. With its new role in the world, it seemed the United States was offered unlimited potential, where progress was impeded only by the limits of man's own imagination. Blinded by the wealth that industrialization produced, America's short-sighted vision would create consequences that are still evident nearly 100 years later. Increased pollution, grueling work in factories, and social upheaval are just a few examples of the ramifications of such industrial progress. Hindsight, of course, is 20/20.

TIME, CONTINUITY, AND CHANGE: ORIGINS OF THE REVOLUTION

The following is an example of journalism praising the industrial progress spawned from the revolution. The author, like countless other Americans at the time, endlessly applauds the nation's progress while failing to estimate what will follow in the wake of the Industrial Revolution.

The present century, from an industrial point of view, has been given largely to the development of inventions, the real age of machinery beginning with the discovery of new devices for spinning and weaving textiles. The inception of this age may be given as the year 1760. The progress in the development has been enormous, and yet, instead of being at the end of the régime of machinery, we are probably only at the beginning. The development must and will go on, and the future achievements of inventive genius in the mechanical and chemical sciences must be looked upon as bright, indeed, and as holding out to humanity many of its best boons and most munificent endowments, not only in moral and industrial directions, but also in a greater and more equal diffusion of wealth and all that wealth means. This development constantly reminds us that the future holds the golden age, and not the past. In this thought we necessarily consider the direct and indirect influences which the development of inventions has had upon labor. The influence has been felt in two directions, economically and ethically, and economically in two directions also, but in diametrically opposite ways. First, in the so-called displacement or contraction of labor, and, second, in the expansion of labor or the increased opportunities for remunerative employment. In considering the economical bearing or influence of inventions, we must deal with labor abstractly; but the ethical influence brings the man as a social and political factor under consideration. So the ethics of the question becomes the most prominent feature of any treatment of the influence of inventions upon labor. The displacement or contraction of labor is the most prominent feature when the economical influence of inventions is discussed. It is the gloomy side, and leads the individual man, the one who is practically displaced, to feel that machinery is his enemy. In the manufacture of agricultural implements, in one establishment in one of the western States, only 600 men, with machinery, are now required to do what 2,145 men, without machinery, were formerly required to do; a clear displacement, or contraction, rather, in this particular instance of the labor of 1,545 men—a proportion of 1 to 3.57. The most glaring instance is to be found in cotton-spinning. At the present time, with one pair of self-acting mules having 2,124 spindles, a single spinner, with the assistance of two boys, will produce 55,098 hanks of No. 32 twist in the same time that it formerly took one spinner to produce by the single spindle hand-wheel five banks of like number twist. Taking all processes of cotton manufacture into consideration, it is quite generally agreed by cotton manufacturers that the displacement is in the proportion of 3 to 1. Even under the dispensation of power machinery, the difference is enormous, for, in 1831, in [the United States], the average number of spindles per operative was 25.2; it is now over 72, an increase of 185 per cent. Of course, along with this increase of the number of spindles per operative, there has been an increase of product per operative; this is 145 per cent, so far as spinning alone is concerned. Under the old hand-loom system, a fair adult weaver wove from forty-two to forty-eight yards of common shirting per week. A weaver to-day, attending six power-looms in a cotton factory, can produce 1,500 yards per week. So instances might be multiplied, but in considering them all, it is impossible to ascertain with any mathematical exactness the displacement or contraction of labor. Any estimate is unsatisfactory, but it may be fair to assume that it is in the ratio of two to one. It is great enough to excite apprehension when only this side of the question is considered. But the second economic fact—the expansion of labor—relieves the mind of such apprehension, for an examination of this expansive influence of inventions reveals a most encouraging condition. The people at large, and especially those who work for wages, have experienced three great elements of progress along with the introduction and use of inventions; First, increased wages; second, reduction of working time; third, reduced cost of articles of consumption. In wages and in product the situation is well illustrated in the cotton industry, the first great industry to feel the effects of invention. The ratio of cost per pound for labor in producing common cotton cloth in this country for the year 1828 and 1880 was as 6.77 for the former to 3.31 in the latter year, a reduction of nearly one-half in cost, the ratio of wages for the same period being $2.62 to $4.84. The hand-loom weaver of America never earned much over fifty cents per day, while at present he earns three times this amount; but his earnings have not increased in proportion to the product of his labor. The expansion of labor is fully shown by the increased consumption of great staples used in manufacturing, cotton and iron, for instance. The consumption per capita of iron in 1870 was 105.64 pounds; it rose, in 1890, to 283.38 pounds.

The consumption per capita of steel increased from 46 pounds in 1880, to 144 pounds in 1890. The consumption of raw cotton in 1830 was 5.9 pounds per capita; in 1880, 13.91 pounds, and in 1890 nearly 19 pounds. This enormous per capita increase in these great staples can indicate but one result—the constant enlargement of the opportunities for employment. Some other figures are still more powerful. The increase in population of the United States, from 1860 to 1880, was 56 per cent, while the increase in the total number of persons engaged in all occupation for the same period was nearly 109 per cent. In the decade from 1870 to 1880 alone, the population increased 30.08 per cent, while the number of persons engaged in all occupations increased 39 per cent. These figures alone constitute a complete answer to the other side of the question—the displacement or contraction of labor; but the expansion receives a powerful illustration when the influence of modern inventions is considered. Many such inventions have actually created employment where none existed before their discovery. As instances of this proposition, the whole department of electricity, electric lighting, telegraphic operations, and the telephone are striking examples. Hundreds of thousands of people are brought into employment through such inventions. The invention of Goodyear, by which rubber is made available for wearing apparel, has furnished employment in untold quantity, where none has been displaced; and not only in furnishing employment, but in increasing the comfort and health of the people the influence has been incalculable. Passing to the ethical influence of inventions, it may be said that inventions brought with them a new school of ethics, for machinery is the type and representative of the civilization of this age, embodying as it does, so far as physics and mechanics are concerned, the concentrated, clearly wrought-out thought of the age. Books represent thought; invention is its embodiment. So we are living in the age of mind, intellect, brain; and brain is king, with machinery as his prime minister. It is only natural that, under such sovereignty, invention should not only typify the progress of the race, but also have a clearly marked influence upon the morals of the people—a mixed influence, as men are what we call good or evil, but, on the whole, with the good vastly predominant. Under this influence the working-man has learned that from a rude instrument of toil furnishing simply crude muscular power, he has become an intelligent exponent of hidden laws. He is no longer a muscular power, simply caring only for the contentment of an animal, but is something more, and wants the contentment which belongs to the best environment. In art operations, which belong to the ethical side of life, the influence of inventions has been as great as in the purely economical field; for by its aid the work of our artisans is rapidly making the taste of the people artistic, as trained and inventive skill puts art into wood and metal. The stove manufacturer, in order to meet the demands of the common people, must secure the services of an artist, that the design of the kitchen or parlor-stove he offers for sale shall not offend the artistic eye. The wage-receiver has been taught to enjoy music and literature; to know that he is a political and moral factor. He sees that he has outgrown the purely physiological relation which labor bears to production, and furnishes the developed mental qualities of man.

CHAPTER TWO

SCIENCE, TECHNOLOGY, AND SOCIETY: A CHANGING WORLD

"A Telephonic Conversation"
By Mark Twain
1880

It is hard to imagine in this day of cell phones, faxes, and the Internet that communicating via the simple telephone could be viewed as a novelty. Yet in 1880, only four years after Alexander Graham Bell's first successful communication through a telephone, the great American writer and humorist Mark Twain could still find himself bemused by the simple act of being in the presence of a person talking on the phone. As a renowned observer of American culture, language, and behavior, Twain was the perfect person to illustrate how this new device could be both a wonderful instrument for communication and a source of irritation and inconvenience.

His observations contain both his trademark sense of satire as well as his honest amazement at the social changes this device had the potential to bring about.

———□———

I consider that a conversation by telephone—when you are simply sitting by and not taking any part in that conversation—

is one of the solemnest curiosities of this modern life. Yesterday I was writing a deep article on a sublime philosophical subject while such a conversation was going on in the room. I notice that one can always write best when somebody is talking through a telephone close by. Well, the thing began in this way. A member of our household came in and asked me to have our house put into communication with Mr. Bagley's, down town. I have observed, in many cities, that the sex always shrink from calling up the central office themselves. I don't know why, but they do. So I touched the bell, and this talk ensued: —

Central Office. [Gruffly.] Hello!
I. Is it the Central Office?
C. O. Of course it is. What do you want?
I. Will you switch me on to the Bagleys, please?
C. O. All right. Just keep your ear to the telephone.

Then I heard, *k-look*, *k-look*, *k'look—klook-klook-klook-look-look*! then a horrible "gritting" of teeth, and finally a piping female voice: "Y-e-s? [Rising inflection.] Did you wish to speak to me?"

Without answering, I handed the telephone to the applicant, and sat down. Then followed that queerest of all the queer things in this world,—a conversation with only one end to it. You hear questions asked; you don't hear the answer. You hear invitations given; you hear no thanks in return. You have listening pauses of dead silence, followed by apparently irrelevant and unjustifiable exclamations of glad surprise, or sorrow, or dismay. You can't make head or tail of the talk, because you never hear anything that the person at the other end of the wire says. Well,

I heard the following remarkable series of observations, all from the one tongue, and all shouted,—for you can't ever persuade the sex to speak gently into a telephone: —

Yes? Why, how did *that* happen?
Pause.
What did you say?
Pause.
Oh, no, I don't think it was.
Pause.
No! Oh, no, I didn't mean *that.* I meant, put it in while it is
   still boiling, —or just before it comes to a boil.
Pause.
WHAT?
Pause.
I turned it over with a back stitch on the selvage edge.
Pause.
Yes, I like that way, too; but I think it's better to baste it on
   with Valenciennes or bombazine, or something of that sort.
   It gives it such an air, —and attracts so much notice.
Pause.
It's forty-ninth Deuteronomy, sixty-fourth to ninety-seventh
   inclusive. I think we ought all to read it often.
Pause.
Perhaps so; I generally use a hair-pin.
Pause.
What did you say? [*Aside*] Children, do be quiet!
Pause.
Oh! B flat! Dear me, I thought you said it was the cat!

Pause.

Since *when?*

Pause.

Why, I never heard of it.

Pause.

You astound me! It seems utterly impossible!

Pause.

Who did?

Pause.

Good-ness gracious!

Pause.

Well, what *is* this world coming to? Was it right in *church?*

Pause.

And was her *mother* there?

Pause.

Why, Mrs. Bagley, I should have died of humiliation! What did they *do?*

Long pause.

I can't be perfectly sure, because I haven't the notes by me; but I think it goes something like this: te-rolly-loll-loll, loll lolly-loll-loll, O tolly-loll-loll-*lee-ly-li-i-do!* And then *repeat,* you know.

Pause.

Yes, I think it *is* very sweet, —and very solemn and impressive, if you get the andantino and the pianissimo right.

Pause.

Oh, gum-drops, gum-drops! But I never allow them to eat striped candy. And of course, they *can't,* till they get their teeth, any way.

Pause.

What?

Pause.

Oh, not in the least,—go right on. He's here writing,—it doesn't bother *him*.

Pause.

Very well, I'll come if I can. [*Aside.*] Dear me, how it does tire a person's arm to hold this thing up so long! I wish she'd—

Pause.

Oh, no, not at all; I *like* to talk, —but I'm afraid I'm keeping you from your affairs.

Pause.

Visitors?

Pause.

No, we never use butter on them.

Pause.

Yes, that is a very good way; but all the cook-books say they are very unhealthy when they are out of season. And *he* doesn't like them, any way, —especially canned.

Pause.

Oh, I think that is too high for them; we have never paid over fifty cents a bunch.

Pause.

Must you go? Well, *good*-by.

Pause.

Yes, I think so. Good-by.

Pause.

Four o'clock, then—I'll be ready. *Good*-by.

Pause.

Thank you ever so much. *Good*-by.

Pause.

Oh, not at all!—just as fresh—*Which*? Oh, I'm glad to hear you say that. *Good*-by.

[Hangs up the telephone and says, "Oh, it *does* tire a person's arm so!"]

A man delivers a single brutal "Good-by," and that is the end of it. Not so with the gentle sex,—I say it in their praise; they cannot abide abruptness.

"The Success of the Electric Light"
By Thomas A. Edison
1880

Thomas Alva Edison, the Wizard of Menlo Park, began work on a viable means of producing incandescent electric light in 1877. Already famous for such inventions as the phonograph, the electric pen (an early means of copying documents), a transmitter that improved the telephone, and numerous improvements to the telegraph, Edison believed that incandescent electric light would not only be a more efficient, safer, and better artificial light to work by than the gas lamps currently in use but cheaper as well.

Working on the problem in his New Jersey lab with his numerous assistants, Edison developed the project for two years before finally coming up with a practical solution. He then went on to promote the new technology and the direct current electrical generation plant on which it was run, eventually winning new investors and, in 1881, permission from the New York City Council to run wires under the city's streets to give electric lights to buildings.

Edison's belief in the viability of incandescent lighting would soon be proved more than justified. However, his belief that powering his new invention with direct current from the generating system he invented was challenged by, among others, George Westinghouse, an inventor and industrialist who saw that Edison's direct current was not able to maintain its power when transmitted over long distances. The 1893 World's Fair in Chicago gave Westinghouse the chance to prove his theories when he beat out Edison for the contract as the fair's electricity provider. The resounding success of the fair proved Westinghouse correct, but despite this defeat, Edison would continue to make advances in various technologies. Edison would become known as the country's most prolific inventor with more than 1,000 patents to his name.

Not a little impatience has been manifested by the public at the seemingly unaccountable tardiness with which the work of introducing the "carbon-loop" electric lamp into general use has hitherto progressed. It is now several months since the announcement was made through the newspapers that all the obstacles in the way of the utilization of the electric light as a convenient and economical substitute for gaslight had been removed: that a method had been invented by which electricity for light or for power could be conveyed to considerable distances economically; that the current could be subdivided almost ad infinitum; and that the electric lamp was henceforth to be as manageable for household purposes as a gas-jet. But, so far as the public can see, the project has since that time made no appreciable advance toward realization. The newspapers have reported, on the whole with a very fair degree of accuracy, the results of the experiments made with this system of lighting at Menlo Park; scientific experts have published their judgments, some of them pronouncing this system to be the desiderated practical solution of the problem of electrical lighting which has vexed the minds of physicists since the day when Sir Humphry Davy produced his famous five-inch voltaic arc. Still it must be confessed that hitherto the "weight of scientific opinion" has inclined decidedly toward declaring the system a failure, an impracticability, and based on fallacies. It will not be deemed discourteous if we remind these critics that scientific men of equal eminence pronounced ocean steam-navigation, submarine telegraphy, and duplex telegraphy, impossibilities down to the day when they were demonstrated to be facts. Under the circumstances, it was very natural that the unscientific public should begin to ask whether they had not been imposed upon by the inventor himself, or hoaxed by unscrupulous newspaper reporters.

Now, the fact is, that this system of electrical lighting was from the first all that it was originally claimed to be, namely, a practical solution of the problem of adapting the electric light to domestic uses and of making it an economical substitute for gaslight. The delays which have occurred to defer its general introduction are chargeable, not to any defects since discovered in the original theory of the system or in its practical working, but to the enormous mass of details which have to be mastered before the system can go into operation on a large scale, and on a commercial basis as a rival of the existing system of lighting by gas.

With the lamp and generator which at the time of the first announcement it was proposed to use, the electric light could have been made available for all illuminating purposes as gas is now; the expense would have been considerably less with the electric light; the lamp would have been quite as manageable as a gas-burner. But, fortunately, the unavoidable delay interposed by administrative and economic considerations afforded opportunity for further research and experiment, and the result has been to introduce many essential modifications at both ends of the system—both in the generator and in the lamp; at the same time sundry important changes, all in the direction of economy and simplification, have been made at almost every point in the system, as well as in the details of manufacturing the apparatus.

With these and other modifications of the system, which need not be particularized here, it may be safely affirmed that the limit of economy, simplicity, and practicability has been reached. The time for experiment has passed; any further improvements to be made in the system must be suggested by its performance when put to the test of actual use on a large scale.

To the question which is so often asked, When will a public demonstration of the working of this system be made? we would reply that such a demonstration will in all probability be made at Menlo Park within two months from this date. The time which has elapsed since the preliminary demonstration of last January has been by no means a season of inaction for the promoters of this enterprise. There is a vast gulf between the most successful laboratory experiment possible and the actualization of the results of that experiment in a commercial sense. A prodigious amount of work was necessitated by the establishment of factories for producing the lamps, the generators, and the other essential parts of the system in large quantities, so as to be able to supply the first demand. We were about to enter a field that was practically unexplored, and, even on a preliminary survey, problems of the most complex kind arose on every side. These had to be solved before the first step could be taken toward the actual introduction of the light into our cities as a substitute for gas. The practical engineer and the man of business can best appreciate the difficulties that had to be overcome. Like difficulties have in the past retarded the general introduction of nearly all the great mechanical and chemical inventions. Years intervened between the discovery of photography and the taking of the first photograph; the steam-engine, the steamboat, the locomotive-engine, did not come till long years after the discovery of their scientific principles; the same is true of the telegraph.

But preparations are being actively made for placing this system of electric lighting within reach of the people in all the great centers of population throughout the United States. To this end, cities are being mapped and divided into districts, each to be supplied with electricity from a central station; estimates are being made of the exact cost of plant in the different cities; contracts are being negotiated for the manufacture on a large scale of engines, dynamos, lamps, wire, and all the other supplies needed for the practical introduction of the system throughout the country; men are being trained to put up the plant of central stations, to run the machines, and to execute all the details of the introduction and working of the system.

A very important question is that of the cost of this light. The price of the electric light will, of course, be determined by the capitalists who invest their money in it as a business venture, but it will of necessity be low as compared with gaslight, though it will vary according to the original cost of plant, the demand in any given locality, and other conditions. It is not at present the intention of the company controlling the patents on this system to supply the light directly to consumers. The company will erect the first station in New York City, and will themselves conduct that station; but the other stations in New York, as well as in the other cities throughout the United States, will be managed by local companies, who will pay a royalty to the Electric Light Company for the right to use the system.

So much can be safely affirmed, that this light can be sold at a price which will make competition on the part of the gaslight companies impossible: 1. Because the total investment in plant to develop a given quantity of light is much less; 2. Because the depreciation of plant is much less; 3. Because the cost for labor employed in very much less than in gas-works; 4. Because the electric-light companies will not have to make any dead investment in large areas of real estate; it is not even necessary to erect buildings specially to serve as stations, for the ordinary buildings, such as are used for different branches of manufacture, will serve the purpose, and may be hired on rental; 5. Because the companies can sell electricity for two uses—for light at night, and for power in the daytime. It has been ascertained by experiment that power can be supplied through this system from twenty-five-horse power down to 1/100 of a horse-power on the same mains that supply the light, and that elevators, printing-presses, sewing-machines, fans, pumps, etc., can be run by electricity from a central station far more economically than by any other means. A canvass of the city of New York has shown that the demand for small powers, in private dwellings and minor industrial establishments, will give occupation to the central stations in the lower part of the city for ten hours daily. This power can be supplied at such a profit to the companies as to more than cover the expense of running the stations for six hours longer in producing electric light. It is evident, therefore, that, in a competition with gas, the electric light possesses an enormous advantage.

"The Progress of Invention During the Past Fifty Years"
By Edward W. Byrn
1896

The last half of the twentieth century saw a tremendous jump in the pace of technological change. From the invention of the jet airliner and the launching of manned rockets to the moon, to the decoding of the human genome and the invention of the semiconductor, the world has seen an incredible increase in productivity and the ability to share information that has been revolutionary to the cultures of the United States and the rest of the world. Only time will tell what effects, both ill and good, the "Second Industrial Revolution" will have on the world.

At the dawn of the twentieth century, changes in technology had also vastly rearranged much of the physical, social, and economic landscapes of the United States. Like moths to a flame, social commentators could not resist attempts at placing the Industrial Revolution in historical context—even as it was happening. The following piece by Edward W. Byrn was typical of the time as it simultaneously dissects the impact of industrialization while predicting what the future holds.

———◻———

If the life of man be threescore years and ten, fifty years will about mark the span of ripe manhood's busy labor, and the sage of to-day, turning back the pages of memory, may, as the times pass in review, enjoy the rare privilege of personal observation of, direct contact with, and positive knowledge concerning the events of this prolific period. To him what a vista it must present; what a convergence of the perspective; for the past fifty years represents an epoch of invention and progress unique in the history of the world. It is something more than a merely normal growth or natural development. It has been a gigantic tidal wave of human ingenuity and resource, so stupendous in its magnitude, so complex in its diversity, so profound in its thought, so fruitful in its wealth, so beneficent in its results, that the mind is strained and embarrassed in its effort to expand to a full appreciation of it. Indeed, the period seems a grand climax of discovery, rather than an increment of growth. It has been a splendid, brilliant campaign of brains and energy, rising to the highest achievement amid the most fertile resources, and conducted by the strongest and best equipment of modern thought and modern strength.

The great works of the ancients are in the main mere monuments of the patient manual labor of myriads of workers, and can only rank with the buildings of the diatom and coral insect. Not so with modern achievement. This last half century has been peculiarly an age of ideas and conservation of energy, materialized in practical embodiment as labor-saving inventions, often the product of a single mind, and partaking of the sacred quality of creation.

The old word of creation is, that God breathed into the clay the breath of life. In the new world of invention mind has breathed into matter, and a new and expanding creation unfolds itself. The speculative philosophy of the past is but a too empty consolation or short-lived, busy man, and, seeing with the eye of science the possibilities of matter, he has touched it with the divine breath of thought and made a new world.

It is so easy to lose sight of the wonderful, when once familiar with it, that we usually fail to give the full measure of positive appreciation to the great things of this great age. They burst upon our vision at first like flashing meteors; we marvel at them for a little while, and then we accept them as facts, which soon become so commonplace and so fused into the common life as to be only noticed by their omission.

Perhaps then, it will serve a better purpose to contrast the present conditions with those existing fifty years ago. Reverse the engine of progress, and let us run fifty years into the past, and practically we have taken from us the telegraph, the sewing machine, the bicycle, the reaper and vulcanized rubber goods. We see no telephone, no cable nor electric railways, no electric light, no photo-engraving, no photo-lithographing nor snapshot camera, no gas engine, no web perfecting printing press, no practical woodworking machinery nor great furniture stores, no passenger elevator, no asphalt pavement, no steam fire engine, no triple expansion steam engine, no Giffard injector, no celluloid, no barbed wire fence, no time lock for safes, no self-binding harvester, no oil nor gas wells, no ice machines nor cold storage. We lose the phonograph and graphophone, or engines, stem winding watches, cash registers and cash carriers, the great suspension bridges, iron frame buildings, monitors and heavy ironclads, revolvers, torpedoes, magazine guns and Gatling guns, linotype machines, all practical typewriters, all pasteurizing, knowledge of microbes or disease germs, and sanitary plumbing, water gas, soda water fountains, air brakes, coal tar dyes and medicines, nitro-glycerine, dynamite and guncotton, dynamo electric machines, aluminum ware, electric locomotives, Bessemer steel, with its wonderful developments, ocean cables, etc. The negative conditions of that period extend into such an appalling void that we stop short, shrinking from the thought of what it would mean to modern civilization to eliminate from its life these potent factors of its existence.

As the issue of patents in this country is based upon novelty, it will aid us in the efforts to appreciate this great movement to note the increase of United States patents in the past fifty years . . .

Within the first decade (1846–1856) came the sewing machine, Bain's chemical telegraph, the Suez Canal, the House printing telegraph, the McCormick reaper, the discovery of the planet Neptune, the Corliss engine, the collodion and dry plate processes in photography, the Ruhmkorff coil, the Bass time lock for safes, the electric fire alarm of Channing & Farmer, Gintle's duplex telegraph, the sleeping car of Woodruff, Wilson's four-motioned feed for the sewing machine, Ericsson's hot air engine, the Niagara suspension bridge, and the building of the Great Eastern [Railway].

The next decade (1856–1866) brought with it the Atlantic cable, the discovery of the aniline dyes by Perkin, the making of paper pulp from wood, the discovery of coal oil in the United States, the invention of the circular knitting machine, the Giffard injector, for supplying feed water to steam boilers; the discovery of caesium, rubidium, indium and thallium; the McKay shoe sewing machine, Ericsson's ironclad monitor, Nobel's explosive gelatine, the Whitehead torpedo, and the first embodiment of the fundamental principles of the dynamo electric generator by Hjorth, of Denmark.

The next decade (1866–1876) marks the beginning of the most remarkable period of activity and development in the history of the world. The perfection of the dynamo, and its twin brother the electric motor, by Wilde, Siemens, Wheatstone, Varley, Farmer, Gramme, Brush, Weston, Edison, Thomson, and others, soon brought the great development of the electric light and electric railways. Then appeared the Bessemer process of making steel; dynamite; the St. Louis bridge; the Westinghouse air brake; and the middlings purifying and roller processes in milling. That great chemist and probably greatest public benefactor, Louis Pasteur, added his work to this period; the Gatling gun appeared; great developments were made in ice machines and cold storage equipments; machines for making barbed wire fences; compressed air rock drills and the Mont Cenis tunnel; pressed glassware; Stearns duplex telegraph, and Edison's quadruplex; the cable car system of Hallidie, and the Janney car coupler; the self-binding reaper and harvester; the tempering of steel wire and springs by electricity; the Lowe process for making water gas; cash carriers for stores; and machines for making tin cans.

With the next decade (1876–1886) there arose a star of the first magnitude in the constellation of inventions. The railway and telegraph had already made all people near neighbors, but it remained for the Bell telephone to establish the close kinship of one great talkative family, in constant intercourse, the tiny wire, sentient and responsive to the familiar voice, transmitting the message with tone and accent unchanged by the thousands of miles of distance between. Then come in order the hydraulic dredges, and Mississippi jetties of Eads; the Jablochkoff electric candle; photography by electric light; the cigarette machine; the Otto gas engine; the great improvement and development of the typewriter; the casting of chilled car wheels; the Birkenhead and Rabbeth spinning spindles; and enameled sheet iron ware for the kitchen. Next the phonograph of Edison appears, literally speaking for itself, and reproducing human speech and all sounds with startling fidelity. Who can tell what stores of interesting and instructive knowledge would be in our possession if the phonograph had appeared in the ages of the past, and the records had been preserved.

The voices of our dead ancestors, of Demosthenes and Cicero, and even of Christ himself speaking, he spake unto the multitude, would be an enduring reality and a precious legacy. In this decade we also find the first electric railway operated in Berlin; the development of the storage battery; welding metals by electricity; passenger elevators; the construction of the Brooklyn bridge; the synthetic production of many useful medicines, dyes, and antiseptics, from the coal-tar products; and the Cowles process for manufacturing aluminum.

In the last decade (1886–1896) inventions in such great numbers and yet of such importance have appeared that selection seems impossible without doing injustice to the others. The graphophone; the Pullman and Wagner railway cars and vestibuled trains; the Harvey process of annealing armor plates; artificial silk from pyroxyline; automobile or horseless carriages; the Zalinski dynamite gun; the Mergenthaler linotype machine, moulding and setting its own type, a whole line at a time, and doing the work of four compositors; the Welsbach gas burner; the Krag-Jorgensen rifle; Prof. Langley's aerodrome; the manufacture of acetylene gas from calcium carbide; the discovery of argon; the application of the cathode rays in photography by Roentgen; Edison's fluoroscope for seeing with the cathode rays; Tesla's discoveries in electricity, and the kinetoscope, are some of the modern inventions which still interest and engage the attention of the world, while the great development in photography, and of the web perfecting printing press, the typewriter, the modern bicycle, and the cash register is beyond numeration or adequate comment.

Looking at this campaign of progress from an anthropological and geographical standpoint, it is interesting to note who are its agents and what its scene of action. It will be found that almost entirely the field lies in a little belt of the civilized world between the 30th and 50th parallels of latitude of the western hemisphere and between the 40th and 60th parallels of the western part of the eastern hemisphere, and the work of a relatively small number of the Caucasian race under the benign influences of a Christian civilization.

Remembering, furthermore, that most of this great development is of American authorship, does it not appear plain that all this marvelous growth has some correlation that teaches an important lesson? Why should this mighty wave of civilization set in at such a recent period, and more notably in our own land, when there have been so many nations far in advance of us in point of age? The answer is to be found in the beneficent institutions of our comparatively new and free country, whose laws have been made to justly regard the inventor as a public benefactor, and the wisdom of which policy is demonstrated by the growth of this period, amply proving that invention and civilization stand correlated—invention the cause and civilization the effect.

This retrospect, necessarily cursory and superficial, brings to view sufficient of the great inventions as milestones on the great roadway of progress to inspire us with emotions of wonder and admiration at the resourceful and dominant spirit of man. Delving into the secret recesses of the earth, he has tapped the hidden supplies of Nature's fuel, has invaded her treasure house of gold and silver, robbed Mother Earth of her hoarded stores, and possessed himself of her family record, finding on the pages of geology sixty millions of years existence. Peering into the invisible little world, the infinite secrets of microcosm have yielded their fruitful and potent knowledge of bacteria and cell growth. With telescope and spectroscope he has climbed into limitless space above, and defined the size, distance and constitution of a star millions of miles away. The lightning is made his swift messenger, and thought flashes in submarine depths around the world, the voice travels faster than the wind, dead matter is made to speak, the invisible has been revealed, the powers of Niagara are harnessed to do his will, and all of Nature's forces have been made his constant servants in attendance. We witness a new heaven and a new earth, contemplation of which becomes oppressive with the magnitude and grandeur of the spectacle, and involuntarily we find ourselves asking the question, "Is it all done? Is the work finished? Is the field of invention exhausted?" It does seem that it is quite impossible to again equal the great inventions of this wonderfully prolific epoch; but as these great inventions, which now seem commonplace to us, would have seemed quite impossible to our ancestors, we may indulge the hope of future possibilities beyond any present conception, but onward and upward in the great evolution of human destiny.

Rejoicing in our strength and capabilities, the new light of man's power and destiny breaks more clearly over us, and content with the infinite quality of mind and matter, the teachings of philosophy, and the facts of evolution, we rest in the assurance of positive knowledge that all that has been done in the past is merely preliminary, that human ingenuity knows no limit, and so long as man himself remains hedged about with the limitations of mortality and the conditions of growth, so long will his strivings and attainments be infinite.

CHAPTER THREE

PEOPLE, PLACES, AND ENVIRONMENTS: FACES OF THE REVOLUTION

"The Right to Work"
By Ray Stannard Baker
1903

The Industrial Revolution produced incredible wealth for those who owned the mines and factories that the new technology made more productive. Those who worked in them, however, had to toil incredibly long hours for low wages without safety nets such as health insurance or compensation in case they were injured or became sick. This led to the rise of various labor unions, which were attempts by the workers to gain some measure of power and stability in order to force the factory owners to treat them more fairly. Not all workers, however, believed that a union was in their best interests. Some workers, as a result of the economic hardships they faced, needed jobs regardless of the wages or conditions and did not want to get caught up in political or social conflicts that would jeopardize their ability to bring in money.

Others, because of their own skills or abilities, were able to individually negotiate better wages or situations with their employers, and they feared that a union would hamper *their ability to get the best deal for themselves. In fact, this was the argument that the owners made when they urged the rejection of unions. The union organizers felt that this was a tactic to divide the workers, arguing that the owners would be able to pit workers against each other to prevent any improvements. These divisions within labor could, especially when a union was trying to organize a company or initiate a strike, lead to violence that disrupted entire communities. The following excerpt from an article in* McClure's *magazine shows just how vicious these internal disputes could become.*

———□———

Public opinion seems to be coming around to the view that the trades' union is here to stay. From many unexpected quarters we hear every now and then a more generous acknowledgment that the organization of labor is not only as inevitable as the combination of capital, but a good thing in itself. At the same time, and from the same fair minds, you hear expressions of passionate indignation at the abuse of power by unions. This means that public opinion is beginning to distinguish between unionism and the sins of unionists, as it is between organized capital and the sins of capitalists.

Clear-headed labor leaders say that violence hurts the union cause, and they denounce it in general. In general, too, violence of the old brick-throwing sort has decreased. It has not disappeared, however, but has taken on a subtler, more deliberate, more terrible form, in many cases, nowadays. Consequently, conditions arise which make liberty and the pursuit of happiness, not to speak of life itself, well nigh impossible to certain of the strikers' fellow men and citizens. The public at large, and often the leaders of unions, do not realize these conditions But it is manifestly the duty of both to understand them clearly.

We believe that the presentation of the facts—the conditions under which the seventeen thousand non-striking miners worked—will be helpful to the public, which is the final arbiter, and beneficial to those also who have in charge the administration of labor unions. Mr. Baker was, therefore, asked to make an impartial investigation and report, and the following article is the result.

—The Editor

How Gorman Was Called Out

Another non-union engineer whom I called on in his engine house was J. R. Gorman, of Exeter Shaft, West Pittston, who had worked for the company twenty-five years. As he said, he was a "free born American citizen, not a made citizen." This is his story:

"At the beginning of the strike Paddy Brann, the president of the local union, came to me and said he was requested to inform me that my presence would be required at St. Alban's Hall that evening to discuss the strike.

"'I can't go,' I said, 'I'm working.'

"'You understand,' he said, 'that when the strike is over you won't have no work.'

"'Won't I?' I said.

"'No sir; we'll see to that, and you won't be able to buy any goods at the store. We'll boycott you.'

"'Partner,' I said to him, 'look here. Don't you bother your head about me; you've got troubles enough of your own.'

"They hung me in effigy and hooted me in the street. I had to go armed, but they didn't dare lay hands on me. I stand on my rights. I won't have anyone coming to me and telling me when I am to work and when I am to quit working. I don't join a union because I object to having some Dago I never saw before coming and ordering me to stop work or to go to work again. I can think for myself. I don't need any guardians. What is the object of their union anyway? Why strike, pure and simple, causing all this rioting and trouble. Some labor organizations give their members benefits and insurance, help take care of the sick, and bury the dead. Do the mine workers? Not a bit of it. They pay in their money month after month, the officers draw fat salaries, and by and by they all strike, and begin persecuting and assaulting honest men who want to work."

Struggles of the Snyder Family

At Wilkesbarre I met John Snyder, a non-striking worker, and his wife. Snyder is a strong-built young fellow, brought up in the coal regions, a fireman by trade, though he never had worked in the mines until this summer. His wife had been a shopgirl in New York City. Just before the strike began she inherited a legacy of $450.

"When we got that," she said, "we thought that now we could have a little home of our own—I mean we could start one."

But the legacy was small, and homes were costly, so Mrs. Snyder finally went out of the city to Stanton Hill, and bought a lot in a miners' neighborhood, paying $100 for it.

Then her husband and his father built a house, mostly of second-hand lumber, leaving the plastering until Snyder should be able to save something from his wages. There was now just money enough left to furnish the house meagerly, and they moved into it, with what joy one may imagine. At last they had a place, a home, in the world. Mrs. Snyder bought a hive of bees, her husband fitted up a chicken-house and made a little garden, hoping thus to add to their income and make the life of their children more comfortable. Every penny they possessed was expended on the home. But Snyder was an industrious fellow, did not "touch, taste, nor handle," as his wife told me, and they knew that he could easily earn enough to support them comfortably.

In the meantime, however, the great strike was on, and every sort of job not connected with the mines was seized upon by union men who were willing to work for almost nothing while the strike lasted, so that Snyder, in order that his family might not be reduced to starvation, was forced, as he told me, to go to work in the mines. He had been thus employed barely four days when one of his neighbors—an Irish striker—came to him. Snyder thus reported to me the conversation which ensued:

"'You're working, are you?'

"'No,' I said.

"'We've got spies on you, and we find that you're firing at the Dorrance.'

"'I am a citizen,' I said, 'and I have a right to work where I please.'

"'Well, I tell you,' he said, 'you can't scab and live here.

You ought to be killed, and you'll find your house blown up some morning if you don't quit.'

"Then a big crowd gathered, mostly Irish, and began to yell 'Scab! Kill him! Kill him!' and throw stones at me. I jumped on my bicycle and escaped."

Snyder now remained within the stockade at the Dorrance colliery day and night, fearing death if the strikers caught him, leaving his wife and two babies in the new home on the hill, not dreaming that any harm would come to defenceless women. But crowds, both grown men and boys, gathered daily under the trees near the house, and every time Mrs. Snyder appeared they hooted at her, often insultingly, sometimes threateningly. After a few days of this treatment she became so fearful of personal injury—for she had seen more than one account in the newspapers of what had happened to the wives of non-striking workers—that she took her babies and, having not even money enough to pay car-fare, fled to the city, where she found shelter for the night. For several days she returned to her home to feed the chickens and look after the bees, always subjected coming and going to the jeers and insults of her neighbors. One day she found that her bees had swarmed, and that the swarm was attached to a near-by tree. Here was the first of the increase. She tried her best to get them down and rehived, but, not strong and a woman, she could not do it. Venturing even insult, she ran out to the men on the hill asking help. Not a man of them would assist her. Instead, they hooted her back to her home, and presently she saw her bees rise and disappear to the hills. She could not tell this part of the story without a quivering lip and a tearful eye.

Those that I have set down here are not chosen as especially flagrant cases; they constitute only a few among scores, even hundreds, of similar tragedies of the great coal strike.

"Child Labor Accounts" 1833

As the factory system began to take shape in England, the birthplace of the Industrial Revolution, the need for more and more laborers to run the relentless machinery became apparent. Partially because of demographics, but also the economic fact that they would command lower wages, children became essential workers in England's factories and textile mills. Often working for slave wages, children as young as ten years old would spend up to sixteen hours a day in the mills, thereby having no time to receive an education or even proper rest. By 1833, a large movement to reform the system grew and the Factory Act was passed, which, while only applicable to children in textile mills, did limit to nine the number of hours that children under the age of thirteen could work.

While the following testimony is taken from England during this first serious attempt to reform child labor, the scenes described would be repeated in the United States as industrialization began to blossom there. In the 1880s, with the start of mass immigration waves from southern and eastern Europe, the number of child workers skyrocketed. While individual states would try at various times to tackle the abuses inherent in this system, it wasn't until the 1941 Supreme Court ruling upholding the 1938 passage of the

Fair Labor Standards Act that the federal government successfully handled the issue at a national level.

When the Industrial Revolution brought factories to England, thousands of little boys and girls, sometimes not more than five or six years old, were employed in tending the machines. Their wages were often merely a pittance, and their hours of work long enough to have worn out even strong adults. Even before the close of the eighteenth century the attention of philanthropists was drawn to the miserable condition of mill workers, and reformers began to urge upon Parliament the necessity of making special provisions to safeguard the health and welfare of the children. In order to learn the real state of affairs, Parliament from time to time appointed commissioners, whose voluminous reports revealed the actual condition of the little workers in the mills.

Charles Harris, a boy working in the carding room of Mr. Oldacres's mill for spinning worsted yarn, testified as follows:

I am twelve years old. I have been in the mill twelve months. I attend to a drawing machine. We begin at six o'clock and stop at half past seven. We don't stop work for breakfast. We do sometimes. This week we have not. Nothing has been said to me by Mr. Oldacres or the overlooker, or anybody else, about having any questions asked me. I am sure of that. The engine always stops for dinner. It works at tea time in the hot weather; and then we give over at half past seven instead of eight, which is the general time. We have generally about twelve hours and a half of it. On Saturdays we begin at six and give over at four. I get 2s. 6d. [two shillings, 6 pennies] a week. I have a father and mother, and give them what I earn. I have worked overhours for two or three weeks together about a fortnight since. All the difference was, we worked breakfast time and tea time, and did not go away till eight. We are paid for such overhours at the rate of 2d. for three hours. I have always that for myself.

What do you do with it?

I save it for clothes sometimes. I put it into a money club for clothes. I have worked nine hours over in one week. I got for that 5 1/2 d. I gave it my mother, and she made it up to 6d. and put it into the money club. She always puts by 6d. a week from my wages for that.

Then your mother gets what you earn by the overhours, don't she?

No; I gets it for myself.

Do you work overhours or not, just as you like?

No; them as works must work . . .

If overhours are put on next week, shall you be glad or sorry?

It won't signify. I shall be neither glad nor sorry. Sometimes mother gives me a halfpenny to spend.

What do you do with it?

I saves it to buy shoes. Have never saved above a shilling for that; mother put more to it, and bought me a pair . . .

Don't you play sometimes after work's over?

Yes, sometimes.

Well, are you not sorry to lose that?

No, I don't mind about it. I am quite sure I don't. I am sometimes tired when I have been at work long hours. I am not tired now; I have been at work all day except dinner; it is now five o'clock. I am sure I had rather work as I do than lose any of my wages. I go to school on a Sunday sometimes. I went first about a month ago. I have been every Sunday since. I can only read in the alphabet yet. I mean to go regular. There is no reason why I should not. I wants to be a scholar.

The father of two children in a mill at Lenton deposed as follows:

My two sons (one ten, the other thirteen) work at Milnes's factory at Lenton. They go at half past five in the morning; don't stop at breakfast or tea time. They stop at dinner half an hour. Come home at a quarter before ten. They used to work till ten, sometimes eleven, sometimes twelve. They earn between them 6s. 2d. [2 shillings, 6 pennies] per week. One of them, the

> eldest, worked at Wilson's for two years, at 2s. 3d. per week. He left because the overlooker beat him and loosened a tooth for him. I complained, and they turned him away for it. They have been gone to work sixteen hours now; they will be very tired when they come home at half past nine. I have a deal of trouble to get 'em up in the morning. I have been obliged to beat 'em with a strap in their shirts, and to pinch 'em, in order to get them well awake. It made me cry to be obliged to do it.
>
> *Did you make them cry?*
>
> Yes, sometimes. They will be home soon, very tired; and you will see them.

I [i.e. the government inspector] preferred walking towards the factory to meet them. I saw the youngest only, and asked him a few questions. He said, "I'm sure I shan't stop to talk to you; I want to go home and get to bed; I must be up at half past five again to-morrow morning."

A family in the same town of Lenton gave the following evidence:

> The boy—*I am going fourteen; my sister is eleven. I have worked in Milnes's factory two years. She goes there also. We are both in the clearing room. I think we work too long hours; I've been badly with it. We go at half past five; give over at half past nine. I am now just come home. We sometimes stay till twelve. We are obliged to work overhours. I have 4s. a week; that is for staying from six to seven. They pay for overhours besides.*

I asked to come away one night lately, at eight o'clock, being ill; I was told, if I went I must not come again. I am not well now. I can seldom eat any breakfast; my appetite is very bad. I have had a bad cold for a week.

Father—*I believe him to be ill from being overworked. My little girl came home the other day cruelly beaten. I took her to Mr. Milnes; did not see him, but showed Mrs. Milnes the marks. I thought of taking it before a magistrate, but was advised to let it drop. They might have turned both my children away. That man's name is Blagg; he is always strapping them children. I shan't let the boy go there much longer; I shall try to apprentice him; it's killing him by inches; he falls asleep over his food at night. I saw an account of such things in the newspapers, and thought how true it was of my own children.*

Mother—*I have worked in the same mills myself. The same man was there then. I have seen him behave shocking to the children. He would take 'em by the hair of the head and drag 'em about the room. He has been there twelve years. There's many young ones in that hot room. There's six of 'em badly now, with bad eyes and sick headache. This boy of ours has always been delicate from a child. His appetite is very bad now; he does not eat his breakfast sometimes for two or three days together. The little girl bears it well; she is healthy. I would prefer their coming home at seven, without additional wages. The practice of working overhours has been constantly pursued at Milnes's factory.*

"A Declaration of Principles"
By Eugene V. Debs
1894

The Pullman Strike of 1894 demonstrated both the power of organized labor and its limitations. The workers of George Pullman's railway car company, as members of the American Railway Union (ARU), initiated the strike in early May in response to large layoffs and wage reductions. The strike soon became national as other railroad workers honored the strike and refused to work on any train with a Pullman car attached. This not only brought the rail traffic to a near standstill, severely damaging the national economy, it also kept mail from being transported. As the strike wore on, this last item became the pretext for the federal government to step in and end the strike. In early July, President Grover Cleveland authorized the use of federal troops to arrest the union's leaders, and by August the strike was over.

The union leader who led the strike and fully recognized the consequences of its outcome was Eugene V. Debs. At first urging the ARU to continue negotiating when it chose to strike, he used his considerable skills as an organizer and public speaker to win sympathy for the workers' cause.

After the Pullman Strike, Debs realized that without effective political power, labor unions would continue to struggle for real power in industrialized America. He ran unsuccessfully as the Socialist Party's candidate for president five times between 1900 and 1920. In 1920, he conducted his candidacy from prison, after being jailed for criticizing the government's persecution of people charged with violating the 1927 Espionage Act. The following piece, published in Debs's Locomotive Firemen's Magazine *shortly after his release from prison for his role in the Pullman strike, hints at his realization that labor must organize and gain a foothold in the hall of government as well as at the bargaining table.*

———□———

In the creation of a new organisation of railway employees, certain reasons prompting the movement are demanded and should be set forth with becoming candour.

The number of employees now in the service of the railroads in America has been variously estimated from 800,000 to 1,000,000. It is safe to assume that this vast army of employees is, at the present time, not less than 1,000,000.

Accepting the highest claims of the various railway organisations as a basis of calculation, less than 150,000 of these employees are members of such organisations, leaving more than 850,000 who are not enrolled in the ranks of organised labour.

To state the proposition concisely, organisation is union. It is a self-evident truth that "in union there is strength," and conversely, without union weakness prevails; therefore, the central benefit to be derived from organisation is strength,— power to accomplish that which defies individual effort . . .

It cannot be denied that the policy of present organisations has filled the land with scabs, who swarm in the highways and byways awaiting anxiously, eagerly, the opportunity to gratify their revenge by taking positions vacated by strikers. Thoughtful men have no difficulty in accounting for the failure of railroad strikes. Neither are they at a loss to suggest a remedy. Organised upon correct principles, governed by just laws and animated by unselfish purposes, the necessity for strikes and boycotts among railway employees will disappear . . .

There will be one supreme law for the order with provisions for all classes, one roof to shelter all, each separate and yet all united when unity of action is required. In this is seen the federation of classes which is feasible, instead of the federation of organisations, which has proved to be utterly impracticable. The reforms sought to be inaugurated and the benefits to be derived therefrom, briefly stated, are as follows:

First — The protection of members in all matters relating to wages and their rights as employees is the principal purpose of the organisation. Railway employees are entitled to a voice in fixing wages and determining conditions of employment.

Fair wages and proper treatment must be the return for efficient service, faithfully performed.

Such a policy insures harmonious relations and satisfactory results. The new order, while pledged to conservative methods, will protect the humblest of its members in every right he can justly claim. But while the rights of members will be sacredly guarded, no intemperate demand or unreasonable proposition will be entertained.

Corporations will not be permitted to treat the organisation better than the organisation will treat them. A high sense of honour must be the animating spirit, and even-handed justice the end sought to be attained.

Thoroughly organised in every department, with a due regard for the right wherever found, it is confidently believed that all differences may be satisfactorily adjusted, that harmonious relations may be established and maintained, that the service may be incalculably improved, and that the necessity for strike and lockout, boycott and blacklist, alike disastrous to employer and employee, and a perpetual menace to the welfare of the public, will for ever disappear.

Second — In every department of labour, the question of economy is forced to the front by the logic of necessity. The importance of organisation is conceded, but if it costs more than a working man is able to pay, the benefits to accrue, however great, are barred. Therefore, to bring the expenses of organisation within the reach of all, is the one thing required, a primary question which must be settled before those who stand most in need, can participate in the benefits to be derived.

The expenditures required to maintain subordinate and grand lodges, every dollar which is a tax upon labour, operate disastrously in two ways, first by repelling men who believe in organisation, and second by expelling members because of inability to meet the exactions, and in both of which the much vaunted fraternity feature, it is seen, is based entirely upon the ability to pay dues. In this it is noted that the organisations, as now conducted, are of men, as a general proposition, who have steady work at fair pay, while others less fortunate in these regards, are forced to remain outside to be the victims of uncharitable criticism.

Hence, to reduce the cost to the lowest practicable point is a demand strictly in accord with the fundamental principles of economy.

This reduction of cost, the new organisation proposes to accomplish in a way that, while preserving every feature of efficiency that can be claimed by existing organisations, will so minimise expenses that members will not be forced to seek relief, as is now the case, in the abandonment of organisation. To accomplish this reduction a number of burdens such as grand and subordinate lodges, annual and biennial conventions, innumerable grievance committees, etc., will be eliminated. As these unnecessary features will not exist, the entire brood of taxes necessary to maintain them will be unknown.

Third — The new organisation will have a number of departments, each of which will be designed to promote the welfare of the membership in a practical way and by practical methods. The best thought of working men has long sought to solve the problem of making labour organisations protective, not only against sickness, disability and death, but against the ills consequent upon idleness, and those which follow in its train: hence there will be established an employment department in which it is proposed to register the name of every member out of employment. The department will also be fully informed where work may be obtained. It is doubtful if a more important feature could be suggested. It evidences fraternal regard without a fee, benevolence without alloy.

Fourth — In the establishment of a department of education, a number of important features are contemplated, as, for instance, lectures upon subjects relating to economics, such as wages, expenses, the relations of employer and employee, strikes, their moral and financial aspects, etc. In this connection a daily paper will be established, whose mission it will be to advocate measures and policies in which labour has vital interests, and also the publication of a standard monthly magazine, which will occupy a still broader field in the discussion of questions which engage the attention of the best writers and thinkers of the times.

Fifth — There will be a department designed to promote legislation in the interest of labour, that is to say, the enactment of laws by Legislatures and by Congress, having in view well-defined obligations of employer and employees, such as safety appliances for trains, hours of labour, the payment of wages, the rights of employees to be heard in courts where they have claims to be adjudicated, and numerous others in which partisan politics will play no part, the common good being the animating purpose.

Sixth — In the department of insurance sound business principles will be introduced, something that has not hitherto engaged the serious attention its importance merits. At present insurance entails grievous burdens without corresponding benefits; to lessen the cost while maintaining every security and every benefit, will be the problem the department will solve. It is the purpose to have a life as well as an accident department, both to be optional with the membership.

With this declaration of its purposes and with boundless faith in its conquering mission, the American Railway Union consecrates itself to the great cause of industrial emancipation.

"Where High Wages Begin"
By Henry T. Ford
1914

The fierce and disruptive battles between labor and management in the late nineteenth and early twentieth centuries led to much discussion among the great magnates of commerce on how best to solve the problem. Some thought that they should keep control by using the legal mechanisms in place, such as the injunction and strike-breaking private detectives, to break any unions that sprang up. Others believed that reforms were necessary to prevent the growth of even more radical unions or political parties that would gain popular support and end the capitalist system for good. One of these latter "captains of industry" was Henry Ford, founder of the Ford Motor Company.

Ford's development of novel industrial practices, like the assembly line, and his adoption of the scientific study of how tasks were performed by workers, brought the benefits and pressures of the industrial age to new heights. He believed in building a car that was affordable, as opposed to a luxury item suitable only as a novelty for the wealthy. He eventually championed better wages for workers, predicting that better-paid workers would have the means necessary to purchase his Model Ts. This desire to create a self-sustaining market, and to keep his workmen happy on the job, led him to issue his famous five-dollar-a-day wage pledge in 1914.

———□———

High wages sounds mighty good. That is, to most people. It is true that a few men seem to think that high wages will ruin business. But the majority of people know better than that. The grocer, the clothier, the furniture maker, the boot and shoe man, the banker—all know better.

There are short-sighted men who cannot see that Business is a bigger thing than any one man's interests. Business is a process of give and take, live and let live. It is co-operation between many forces and interests.

Whenever you find a man who believes that Business is a river whose beneficial flow ought to stop as soon as it reaches him, and go no farther to refresh and enrich other men's fields, you find a man who thinks he can keep Business alive by stopping its circulation.

There are some men who, if they got all they wanted, would get everything, and so destroy the very thing they seek. This is lack of vision.

* * *

What do we mean by high wages, anyway?

We mean a higher wage than was paid [ten] months or

ten years ago. We do not mean a higher wage than ought to be paid. Our high wages of today may be low wages ten years from now.

If it is right for the manager of a business to try to make it pay larger dividends, it is just as right that he should try to make it pay higher wages. For wages are the chief dividend—on the money side at least—and more people are dependent on them. But where the commonest mistake is made is here: We sometimes imagine that it is the manager of the business who pays the high wages. Of course, if he can and will not, then the blame is his. But if he can, it is not himself alone that makes it possible.

When you trace it all down to its source, it is really the workmen who earn the wages. Their labor is the productive factor. It is not the only productive factor, of course, for poor management can waste labor just as it can waste material and make it unproductive.

But in a partnership of good management and good labor, it is the workman who makes good wages possible. He invests his energy and skill, and if he makes an honest, whole-hearted investment, good wages ought to be his reward. Not only has he earned them, but he has had a big part in creating them.

* * *

The employer who, in fairness, is paying good wages is not, therefore, to be applauded as an angel. It is not all his doing. If his men did not do their part in making the business productive and profitable, he would not have the big wage to pay. So that the credit is not all his. He is only sharing justly, or nearly so, with the men who were his active partners in the business.

It is not a question of the employer showing his generosity, or playing My Lord Bountiful, or anything like that. It is simply the square deal. And it is the only practical way of keeping a business productive and profitable.

A business whose benefits come to a halt in the company's office is not a healthy business. The benefit has got to circulate so that every man who had a part in creating and running it has also a part in enjoying it. It is simple fairness.

* * *

Paying good wages is not charity at all—it is the best kind of business.

The kind of workman who gives the business the best that is in him is the best kind of workman a business can have. But he cannot be expected to do this indefinitely without proper recognition.

Good wages help keep the good workman a good workman for the sake of the business.

The man who comes to the day's job feeling that no matter how much he may give, it will not yield him enough of a return to keep him beyond the margin of want, is not in shape to do his day's work. He is anxious and worried and it all reacts to the detriment of his work.

But if a man feels that his day's work is not only supplying his basic need, but is also giving him a margin of comfort, and enabling him to give his boys and girls their opportunity and his wife some pleasure in life, then his job looks good to him and he is free to give it his very best.

This is a good thing for him and a good thing for the business. The man who does not get a certain satisfaction out of his day's work is losing the best part of his pay.

Do you know, the day's work is a great thing—a very great thing! It is at the very foundation of our economic place in the world; it is the basis of our self-respect; it is the only way to reach out and touch the whole world of activity.

* * *

All of us are workingmen these days. If we are not, we are parasites. No amount of money excuses any man from working. He is either producer or parasite—take your choice.

All of us don't do the same things, our jobs are different. But all of us are working for the same end, and that end is bigger than any of us.

The employer who is seriously trying to do his duty in the world must be a hard worker. It is useless for him to say, "I have so many thousand men working for me." The fact of the matter is that so many thousand men have him working for them—and the better they work the busier they keep him disposing of their products.

Wages and salaries are in fixed amounts, and this must be so in order to have a basis to figure on. But where the profits exceed these there ought to be profit-sharing. Wages and salaries are a sort of fixed profit-sharing, but it often happens that when the business of the year is closed up it is discovered that more can be done, and then more ought to be done. Where we are all in the business working together, we all ought to have some share in the profits, either a good wage or salary, or added compensation.

* * *

The business man's ambition ought to be to pay the best wages the business can carry, and the workman's ambition should be to respond to make the best wages possible.

A business man sometimes does not know just how to say this. There are men in all shops who seem to believe that when they are urged to do their best, it is for their employer's benefit and not their own. It is a pity that such a feeling should exist. But perhaps there have been enough abuses in the past to justify it in many instances.

If an employer urges men to do their best, and the men learn after a while that their best does not mean any reward for them, then they simply go back into the rut and all the urging is wasted.

But if men follow the urging and do their best, and then see the fruits of it in their pay envelope, it is proof to them that they are an essential part of that business, and that its success largely depends on them. They feel also that there is justice in that business and that their efforts will not be ignored.

* * *

It ought to be clear, however, that the higher wage begins down in the shop. If it is not created there it cannot get into the pay envelopes. It must begin there, and it ought to keep on circulating until a just proportion of it gets back there, and when profit-sharing time comes the men who helped to make the profits should not be forgotten.

So when the workman is urged to do his best, it ought not to be a game that is played on him. His best ought to mean the best for himself as well as for the business. And unless it does mean this his best is going to be hard to get.

It is a sense of fellowship in work that we need. And fair dealing will give it to us. Why do we have these classes of "capital" and "labor" set apart as enemies? Simply because fair dealing has not been the rule. What is "capital" without "labor"? And what is "labor" but "capital"? And what earthly use is "capital" unless it labors and produces the things which life requires?

We must get together on these matters, and the only way we can get together is to begin with fair dealing.

One ounce of fair dealing is worth a ton of fair speeches.

* * *

Every business that employs more than one man is a partnership. This is so whether the man at the head of the business acknowledges it or not.

Suppose a man invents an article which is capable of wide use by the people.

With his own two hands he cannot make enough of them to satisfy the demand. He might work hard all his life and make only a few.

So he gets other men to give their labor that his creation may gain currency in the world. It is still his idea, but they help him to spread it. Without his idea there would not be so many jobs in the world. Without their labor there would not be so many articles of commerce.

You see, the man at the head can no longer say MY business, but all of them together can say OUR business, and when this is the spirit, and it is practiced all the way through, the very best kind of a partnership exists.

There is too much of the "my" and too little of "our," both in the shops and the head office. The workman has got to assume that it is "our" business. It is the only way he can feel that it is "his" business, too.

The source of every productive result is the day's work. That is the seed from which every fruitful crop springs. The farmer gets no more out of the ground than he puts into it by his labor. And it is what the worker puts into the business that makes it pay.

What would any of us be without work? Who is so pitiable as the man without an occupation that contributes something to the life of the trade?

And just as pitiable is the man who drags himself through the day's work as if he were a slave, doing as little as possible, and that little badly.

He is a brake on the wheels of industry. He is lowering its wage-paying power. He is like a faulty machine that costs more than it produces. Multiply him by a sufficient number and the business is ruined—it loses its power to support anybody connected with it.

There will never be a system invented which will do away with the necessity of work. Nature has seen to that. Idle hands and minds were never intended for any one of us. Work is our sanity, our self-respect, our salvation. So far from being a curse, work is the greatest blessing. It is only when it is mixed with indolence or injustice that it becomes a curse.

Take it from a man who has worked from his earliest years, and who is a workingman now, and proud to be one, that no one can get any more out of his job than he puts into it.

CHAPTER FOUR

PRODUCTION, DISTRIBUTION, AND CONSUMPTION: THE IMPACT OF THE REVOLUTION

"Gary, the Magic City"
By Elliott Flower
1909

> The company town played a prominent role in American industrial and labor history. In fact, one of the most modern cities in America, one that took advantage of the early fruits of the exploding industrialization that swept the United States during the Industrial Revolution, was Pullman, Illinois.
> Founded in 1880 by George Pullman, the multi-millionaire and founder of the Pullman Palace Car Company, the town was imagined as a model of cleanliness, with reliable modern services (such as gas for cooking and illumination in each home), and pleasant landscaping. Dreamed up as a modern utopia for the employees of the Pullman Company, these pleasant living conditions were intended to improve morale and productivity among the employees. Economic hardships, the death of George Pullman, and other factors would soon spell the demise of Pullman and its utopian dreams.

> In the spirit of Pullman, the United States Steel Corporation founded Gary, Indiana, as a city for the workers at the gigantic steel mills it finished erecting there in 1909. United States Steel was the giant trust put together by J. P. Morgan, Andrew Carnegie, Elbert Gary, and Charles Schwab. Created in 1901 by the merger of Carnegie Steel with Federal Steel and three other firms, United States Steel quickly dominated the national and world market.
>
> As the Industrial Revolution slowed, and economic opportunities spread to other areas of the country, the vision of Gary began to dim. In recent decades, the town, located just southeast of Chicago, has been mired in economic depression and neglect, remaining as a simple testament to the capricious nature of the capitalist vision and the unrealized utopian dreams of industrialization.

> The United States last year made more steel (over 23,000,000 tons) than Germany, Britain, France and Belgium combined. New steel works are under construction which will produce enough to enable her to make more than the whole world besides. This she will do within five years, probably within three.
>
> —Andrew Carnegie in The Century

This is not the age of magicians, we are told, and yet, judged by ordinary standards, the building of the city that is to enable the United States to fulfill Mr. Carnegie's prophecy must be regarded as something very close to magic, as a brief outline of its history to date and the plans for the future will show.

In June, 1906, the site of Gary, Indiana, some twenty-six miles from Chicago, was a barren waste of drifting sand, with occasional patches of scrub-oak. It had no population, was valueless for agricultural purposes, had no natural harbor or shelter of any kind, and no laden boat could get within a half-mile of the shore. The drifting sand piled up in ever-shifting ridges that buried whatever might lie in its path; three or four railroad lines, intent only on reaching points beyond, crossed it by the shortest possible route; and the Grand Calumet River—grand only in name—wormed a tortuous way in and out among the sand dunes until it finally found Lake Michigan. A gun club was located in the vicinity, and the average man would have said that nothing but a gun club could find any possible use for the land. Then—in June, 1906, remember!—the first spadeful of sand was turned for the new steel town of Gary.

For a long time thereafter there were still no outward indications of the building of a city. Many laborers were there, some housed in tents and some in hastily constructed shacks; but they were digging, digging, digging, in long trenches, and very little work was done above ground. For Gary, unlike the town or city of normal growth, was built from the foundations up. Houses are always so constructed, but it is rarely that a town is built on this plan. In brief, all underground work—the laying of sewers, water pipes, gas mains, electric light conduits, etc.—was done first, and they were laid in what were to be the alleys. The men who planned and built, and are still building, Gary had no mind to have things torn up for any purpose whatever after the buildings were erected and the pavements laid. So they began at the bottom. Some work on the Grand Calumet River, the course of which had to be changed and straightened, was done during this time; three railroads began moving their rights-of-way, so that space for the plant might be left clear; and the dredging of the slip that was to run a mile inland was started. Then, when the underground work was far enough along, the building began.

Now let us see how rapid has been the construction of this magic city, for the rapidity of construction is one of the most amazing things connected with the enterprise. A wonderful city Gary is to be, a model manufacturing city, an attractive city, a city that in its government and individual ownership of business and residence property will be altogether unlike most made-to-order towns; but, in spite of all this, it is the speed with which it has been, and is being, built that commands first attention, and even this cannot be fully appreciated unless one considers the natural obstacles and the character of the buildings. The open-hearth buildings, for instance, are 1189 by 204 feet each, the blast furnaces have a daily capacity of 450 tons each, and virtually all the buildings of the plant are of mammoth size. Moreover, they require the very strongest foundations, so that it would ordinarily require as much time merely to put in the foundations as it would take to complete a building of less solid construction. Again, the temporary housing of the men to build the plant and town required some extra thought and labor, for they had to be carried through one winter without permanent shelter.

Although the plant and town are and will be under the same municipal jurisdiction, they are being built by separate companies, both subsidiary to the United States Steel Corporation, so it is natural and easy to consider them separately, and I shall take up the plant first, the town being merely a necessary adjunct to the plant.

In August, 1907, fourteen months after work was begun, I spent two or three days in Gary, and this was the situation: All underground work was completed, and the water-supply tunnel, extending two miles into the lake, was well out under the waves; the dredges that were making the slip had penetrated a quarter of a mile inland; breakwaters, to protect the slip, already extended some distance out into the lake; the main office building was occupied, although considerable work on the interior remained to be done; the finishing touches were being put on the machine shop, boiler shop, blacksmith shop, pattern and carpenter shop and storehouse; the foundations for the first open-hearth building were in and the iron work about sixty per cent. completed; work on the foundations of the second open-hearth building had been begun; the foundations were in and about seventy per cent. of the iron work completed on the first group of four blast furnaces; work on the second group of four blast furnaces had been begun; the pumping station was about seventy-five per cent. done; the foundations for the electric station were about half completed; twenty per cent. of the foundations of the rail mill were in and the iron work was started; the electric repair shop, pattern warehouse, foundry, roll shop, and blowing engine for the first four blast furnaces were under construction; the foundations for the ore bins were in and construction work begun; one great ore unloader was nearing completion and others were being erected; and the foundations for the ore bridges were being put in.

On July 23, 1908, the steamer E. H. Gary, with the first cargo of iron ore for the plant, poked her nose into the slip, and thereafter the ore bins filled rapidly. On December 21, 1908, just about two and a half years after the first spadeful of sand was turned up, the fire in the first blast furnace was started and steel-making actually began. On that date the superintendent reported the following buildings completed: Four blast furnaces, with boiler house, blowing engine house and gas-cleaning plant; electric power station, central pumping station, two open-hearth buildings, rail mill, locomotive house, foundry, and all shops, including machine shop, roll shop, boiler shop, blacksmith shop, carpenter, and pattern shop, etc. The slip, with its ore unloaders and ore bins, had been in use for some time, and the main office building had been completed and occupied for many months. Buildings then under construction were four blast furnaces, with boiler house, blowing engine house and gas-cleaning plant; pig casting plant, billet mill, and merchant mills. The departments in operation were one blast furnace, the foundry and all the shops, but the opening of other departments would follow naturally and quickly upon the beginning of blast furnace operations.

Turning from the plant to the town, one who knew what the site was originally finds a transformation quite as startling. While the town lacks the tremendous buildings that made the problem of the plant, it had many more structures of one kind or another to put up and many problems of its own to solve. The building of the plant within so short a time was unquestionably the greater undertaking, but, somehow, to find an attractive city of 15,000 population and accommodations for as many more under construction, with trees and lawns and every modern convenience, where there was nothing but sand and scrub-oak before seems more like modern magic than does the plant itself. True, much remains to be done, and you may step into a side street here and there that shows some of the former desolateness or that building operations still keep untidy; or you may wander into The Patch, of which I shall have more to say later, where the steel company has been unable to carry out the plans it made for the rest of the town; but, on the whole, you will be mightily pleased and even more astonished at what you see. Gary has two hotels—one of them as perfect in its appointments as any that you can find in the country,—two banks, a newspaper, a wide street (Broadway) lined with stores and office buildings, an arcade building for the smaller shopkeepers, and many handsome residences. As a matter of fact, you can find almost any kind of a residence you may desire in Gary, excepting only the hovel and the palace; and they are all sightly and well constructed. I am not including The Patch in this description. Every man builds for himself in The Patch without the restrictions that are imposed on those who would build elsewhere in Gary, and it naturally follows that The Patch has structures that would not be tolerated in other parts of the town, although it also has some that are well up to the standard.

Education, both secular and religious, received attention from the very beginning; the need of recreation was recognized and provision has been made for first-class amusements. There are already one large permanent schoolhouse and many temporary ones. The temporary schools, so made that they can be taken apart and moved from place to place, have been a feature of Gary since the commencement of building operations, and they, as well as the construction camps, have been moved as work progressed. A temporary structure, to serve as a sort of universal church where all denominations have equal rights, was erected, and permanent structures are to follow. Sites have been secured and the plans approved for several. The Episcopalians, in addition to their church, will have a building for social gatherings and entertainments, to be known as the Universal Club, and the Roman Catholics have secured sites and prepared plans for a church, a parochial school, and a parish house. A Chicago manager has purchased a site and agreed to build a theatre that is to cost not less than $125,000. For health and recreation, as well as beauty, two parks have been laid out very near the heart of the town, one on either side of Broadway and but a short distance from that thoroughfare. I have endeavored, in this, to give some idea of the marvellous transformation that has taken place in two and one half years, but it is so big a thing that it is difficult to grasp it in its entirety. The building of either plant or town alone in that time would have been a tremendous undertaking, possible only for a corporation having courage and unlimited resources, and to build them together just about doubled the magnitude of the task.

"The Delirium of Dress"
By the Looker-On
1899

The following piece touches on many of the effects that the Industrial Revolution had on culture and society. With the growth of manufacturing and the wealth that it generated, women began to find new opportunities as cultural values began to reflect these changes. Many unmarried women now found work in the cities as stenographers, typists, and other office workers. While women of the privileged class were still expected to remain in the home and manage domestic affairs, especially in Victorian England, changes brought by industrialization meant that a certain freedom became available to women of the new "middle" class.

In the following piece, a male journalist notes these changes, especially how fashion has become a means for women to assert their independence. His tone, a mixture of amusement and disdain, has echoes of a feeling that the new cultural landscape will bring an end to the dominance that men have enjoyed in society and business. This piece captures the very embryonic stages of the middle class in the modern world.

———◻———

For a spectacle of "hollow hearts that wear a mask" there was no better standpoint than the stalls of Covent Garden in 1899 with your face to the audience. Upon the whole, fashionable marriage supplied the greater amount of fluttering excitement this year, perhaps; on the other hand, manicure showed signs of becoming a serious preoccupation. In dining—the ever-superlative function of social life in England, and not a bad one either—a certain evolutionary change appears, and is not unlikely to spread. Revolutionary it might also be called, since it is a return to tavern-dining. Private parties are given at "smart" hotels often enough to suggest the beginning of a vogue. And as a vogue it may pass; yet out of the words "multitude," "money," "convenience," substantial reason for the practice may be grubbed. Of dancing there seems to have been more than the recent average, which, according to many anxious mothers, has been painfully low. In a season of *éclatant* fashionable marriage, such an average naturally tends to rectification. There is stimulus, there is hope. Good-natured women with commodious houses are moved to kindness, and there are one or two more great balls. Yet had there been more dancing this year, and much more, it could not have equalled the very grave demand. But dress!—there we come to the most notable thing of all.

Mr. Winterley, who has on various occasions reported upon what is much more than a pleasure to the eye, being at the same time financial ravage and a torment of hearts, goes back to Sussex out of patience on all scores. No pleasure to the eye, says this social observer, tolerant, urbane, old in bottle—"No pleasure at all, except what the loom and the vat provide. Beautiful tissues in exquisite dyes, fashioned in the taste and sometimes by the hand, apparently, of an upholsterer. Indeed, were there a tolerable synonym of 'upholstered,' that is the word I should choose to describe many a dame of my acquaintance in her newest gown. Even in the designs on these fine stuffs, wherein the Western handicraftsman matches the East at last, there is or was a prevalent curtain-and-cord motif that might have been caught from Gillow's; and it was only too faithfully carried out by the constructionist who made up the material. Another effect was obviously borrowed from the top-hamper of those new-fangled standard lamps; and it is still favorite, though the modes of a season are now the modes of a

PRODUCTION, DISTRIBUTION, AND CONSUMPTION: THE IMPACT OF THE REVOLUTION

month, or perhaps of a week. 'Give me the name of your upholsterer,' I would have said to a dear lady of my acquaintance, only for its offending her too much; but as it certainly would, I did say, 'Give me the name of your dressmaker, for I am distressed in mind and wish to ask her a question.' She naturally inquired what her dressmaker had to do with my distress, and whether she herself could not answer as well. This opened my way. I explained that I was anxious to know whether it was true, as I had read somewhere, that the London dressmakers were all out of their minds before the middle of July with the extraordinary number of gowns they were ordered to supply, their young women being in similar case from want of sleep. If so, whence the demand arose, and what sudden accretion of wealth—which seemed to be general—justified its indulgence. I was at once assured that the answer was quite simple, and that there was nothing in it. On many occasions no one under forty could wear anything but these Liberty muslin sort of stuffs, which were odious if not perfectly fresh, and were done for in no time; so that there was really nothing for it but a larger number of dresses—which after all, were cheap, I was to remember.

"Ah, I know this cheapness. Bachelors with married sisters and modestly inquiring minds, bachelors who are trustees, bachelors who are called in when friends or relatives come to grief—they know. This cheapness is a cheapness that should allow me provision of forty dress-coats a year, with a margin for new socks of the very best spun silk every week. No. There was something in the explanation, no doubt; but I fear me that the full truth could not be confessed even though the bolt was about to be withdrawn, the fatal 'drop' to fall, the lady to be launched into eternity. Mere competition in the brag of spending cannot be avowed and continued with decency. The nearest approach to avowal is made when we hear that one must live up to the times, or to one's neighbors, or to one's social obligations and what is expected of us. But were our multitudinous daughters of luxury to make a clean breast of it, they would confess that, often, where many of them are gathered together in array, it is a *mêlée* in which wounds are given and taken, and triumphs glory and rankle right and left in a silent Donnybrook of the brag of spending. Return to cards as a fashionable vice cannot be recommended *per se*; but whether on comparison of broad results and ultimate consequences, it be not preferable to this other when an equal height of extravagance has been reached, will be an interesting question before long. That the prevalent vice is essentially the more savage, more indulgent of the lower primitive instincts, can be shown at any time, I think. And again, again, again, where does the money come from to supply the game at which so many play? I do not aim the question at the thousand and one miracles of expenditure performed every day, but, more innocently and scientifically, at the gross sum, the money in the lump, the prodigious 'tottle of the whole,' to which even the millionairesses only contribute the price of hats and bonnets and gowns for selves and daughters. What vast extraneous fund supplies without exhaustion the insufficiencies that seem Innumerable to all observers? The National Drink Bill has had its turn, and a very good one. By this time it has been thoroughly examined for all that it can yield to every department of social inquiry. The Dress Bill—"

But the rest of Mr. Winterley's letter is too long to print and it barely touches upon a particularly interesting part of his subject, though he evidently had it in mind.

The man and the woman are one, and yet they are different. They are very dear to each other, but because of their difference each sex has its special privileges, appanages, and assignments in the scheme of companionship, even when the two are so intimately related as to be considered identical. To say "kitchen" and "counting-house" in the same breath, or to imagine the intentional deposit of bonnet-boxes in the smoking-room, sufficiently brings out my meaning. It is difficult to tell why a man should not enter, and frequently enter, a part of his premises in which he has a direct interest daily renewed, but that in doing so he encroaches offensively is agreed; and more delicate understandings are numerous.

By one of these unspoken conventions, the Newspaper has been considered the appanage of Man. Women the most conscious of command at the breakfast-table stop short of appropriating the newspaper. No woman sensitive to the fine yet rigorous delicacies of the domestic condominium ever opens the paper first. Behind his newspaper a man is in retirement: its companionship marks him "private." With the mere net of taking it up he is in his study: that is to say, where Woman enters only by permission, and where the intrusion of bonnet-boxes (were that attempted which till now seemed inconceivable) would be a grievance bordering on outrage.

Now, however, a man's newspaper is no longer his own. He enters it to find the bonnet-boxes there. The milliner herself is in possession, scattering her blouses and vests, her skirts and bodices, her ruches and tuckers, her fichus, her chemisettes, and her chatter, up one column and down another, with exuberant impropriety. An otherwise offensive invasion, it humiliates, we know not why, unless that it makes men feel like Peeping Toms entirely against their will. And it is not as if women hadn't newspapers of their own. There are scores of such, all devoted to attire, and each with separate altars and side-chapels for the *modiste*, the *corsetier*, the *perruquier*, and all concerned as ministers and celebrants of the cult. Nor is it as if the raptures of the toilette were sung in a corner of the newspapers once our own. They are allowed to break out in all directions. A new play being put upon the stage you hasten to read of the first night's performance, and plump into a rhapsodical "description of the dresses." Wading out of that, you leap a long lyric of lovely gowns in the audience, but only to drop into the details of similar "confections" when you turn to the race-course, or scan the news from Henley. There are no popular preachers nowadays, or we should read on Mondays of how Lady A., "sitting immediately under the pulpit, looked delicious in a white *crêpe de Chine* over cerise taffetas; while Lady B. and her girls—" and so forth. Women are not yet admitted to Parliament; when they are, the lady reporter will be there to gem the debates with such records as that "the Hon. Mrs. Coalport (exquisitely gowned in oyster silk, sweetly enriched with godets in *vieux rose* and *bouillonné à merveille* in white chiffon) rose to express her undying hostility" to whatever it was that Mrs. Coalport was hostile to.

But there are ways of looking at the matter which are less of a joke. When so many publications of every grade, some selling in tens of thousands, others at a greater rate, mirror the luxury of fine ladies and reflect the delights of being charmingly dressed; when the demand for this sort of reading seems so wide and eager that the sober publishers of the soberest newspapers have to give way to it; when the dresses on the stage are an acknowledged attraction of the theatre, and every other place of public resort is a show and a study of the same kind, what should we think?

For one thing, we may suspect, perhaps, the original spontaneity of this demand: We may suppose it nursed into flourishing existence by the enterprise of Supply in want of customers, and perceptive of an unworked field of human interest. Women are half the population; and it is an old remark that when they talk together their more sacred converse is ever of him and of it, and that—

Every "he" a sweetheart means,
And every "it" a gown.

The first result of this observation, as it affects printers and publishers, was the love-tale as a commodity; its counterpart had naturally to await the coming of the lady journalist. A man may be a rare designer and an excellent cutter-out; but he has neither the eye to drink, nor the soul to feel, nor the utterance to make known the beauty of a Paris gown. No man, whatever his culture, ever really thrilled to the perfections of a toque or felt the poesy of pure paduasoy—capabilities which every housemaid is born with. Came the lady journalist then, and with her the means of calling forth, cultivating, ministering to, and making a market of the widest range of sensibilities in the female breast, save one alone.

Small blame to the sensibilities. They are as natural and as innocent as those others of which we make romance and song. There is no more harm in loving to look pretty than in loving to be loved; and order and sweetness and other good things come of the desire "still to be neat, still to be dressed." But, like those other sensibilities, they have highly cultivable extremes, and in that condition they make aids and associates of bad, tormenting and tormented passions. That is an old story, of course; but what we speak of is something new. We speak of entirely new provocation to these extremes, and provocation that works several ways at once. The craving for notoriety which is at the same time inspired and gratified by the newspaper press, has overcome the crowd of idle rich women as readily as other folk. To them the lady journalist appears with help to their only way of satisfaction; and, by degrees, her account in the public press of Mrs. B.'s wonderful appearance in one turn-out, the dream of loveliness presented by Lady C. in another, has stimulated a competition of cost and display in dress which has never run so high as this season. But the consequent mischief ends not where it began. It is not only to a few hundreds of fine ladies that the competition appeals. At the same time many wealthy women who hope to figure publicly—that is to say, notoriously—in the world of fashion to which they belong, hear and respond with all their hearts, and with all their souls, and with all their financial strength. These raise the standard of "living up to what is expected of us" for others of the same rank and the same "sets," but with no such command of the wherewithal. Hence much tribulation, much temptation of sorts, soreness of heart incalculable, and all for no real or no substantial cause. And still the mischief spreads, descending from class to class, and in every class afflicting women of small means and no pretentiousness quite as much as any. For a woman need not have much personal vanity to be hurt when she makes a comparatively poor figure in every company she enters. She may even be unhappy without being at all weak or wicked; while as for them that are, they may drop into more unhappiness still, carrying other folk with them. Now, if but a very small percentage of the whole number of women within risk of this social plague were touched by it, the total would not be small; for starting at the apex of society, it is repeated in round after round of an expanding spiral (there are no separate "circles" in our social system) till it ends in the tens of thousands of a lower middle class.

"A Nightly Scene in London"
By Charles Dickens
1856

In England, while the Industrial Revolution brought the promise of wealth and opportunity to many people, a tremendous amount of people in England felt the severe dislocations that happened when the promise of a factory job failed to materialize. As more and more people moved from England's rural areas to the newly industrialized areas such as London and Manchester, they found that there was no support for them if they got sick, were injured, or failed to find employment. In the United States, similar scenes such as this would repeat themselves in urban areas like New York City and Chicago.

Charles Dickens began his career in 1828 as a freelancer for newspapers where he documented the sights and sounds of the new industrial economy that he encountered on the London streets. He was the perfect writer to capture the despair and poverty that these people endured as the complexity of urban life became an increasingly harsh and unwelcoming environment. Dickens would later incorporate the details of London's city life into numerous novels, including Oliver Twist, Great Expectations, *and* Bleak House. *An avid proponent of reform, he hoped that by reading about the conditions of the lower classes in his novels, his readers would be moved to support the creation of some form of a social safety net for the less privileged. He also continued to write as a journalist, and the following piece is an example of his ability to astutely capture both the despair and simple dignity of those the new industrial economy was leaving behind.*

———□———

On the fifth of last November, I, accompanied by a friend well known to the public, accidentally strayed into Whitechapel. It was a miserable evening; very dark, very muddy, and raining hard.

There are many woeful sights in that part of London, and it has been well known to me, in most of its aspects, for many years. We had forgotten the mud and rain in slowly walking along and looking about us, when we found ourselves, at eight o'clock, before the Workhouse.

Crouched against the wall of the Workhouse, in the dark street, on the muddy pavement-stones, with the rain raining upon them, were five bundles of rags. They were motionless, and had no resemblance to the human form. Five great bee-hives, covered with rags—five dead bodies taken out of graves, tied neck-and-heels, and covered with rags—would have looked like those five bundles upon which the rain rained down in the public street.

"What is this?" said my companion. "What is this?"

"Some miserable people shut out of the Casual Ward, I think," said I.

We had stopped before the five ragged mounds, and were quite rooted to the spot by their horrible appearance. Five awful Sphinxes by the wayside, crying to every passer-by, "Stop and guess! What is to be the end of a state of society that leaves us here!"

As we stood looking at them, a decent working-man, having the appearance of a stonemason, touched me on the shoulder.

"This is an awful sight, Sir," said he, "in a Christian country!"

"God knows it is, my friend," said I.

"I have often seen it much worse than this, as I have been going home from my work. I have counted fifteen, twenty, five-and-twenty, many a time. It's a shocking thing to see."

"A shocking thing, indeed," said I and my companion together. The man lingered near us a little while, wished us good-night, and went on.

We should have felt it brutal in us who had a better chance of being heard than the working-man, to leave the thing as it was, so we knocked at the Workhouse gate. I undertook to be spokesman. The moment the gate was opened by an old pauper, I went in, followed close by my companion. I lost no time in passing the old porter, for I saw in his watery eye a disposition to shut us out.

"Be so good as to give that card to the master of the Workhouse, and say I shall be glad to speak to him for a moment."

We were in a kind of covered gateway, and the old porter went across it with the card. Before he had got to a door on our left, a man in a cloak and hat bounced out of it very sharply, as if he were in the nightly habit of being bullied, and of returning the compliment.

"Now, gentlemen," said he, in a loud voice, "what do you want here?"

"First," said I, "will you do me the favor to look at that card in your hand. Perhaps you may know my name."

"Yes," says he, looking at it. "I know this name."

"Good. I only want to ask you a plain question in a civil manner, and there is not the least occasion for either of us to be angry. It would be very foolish in me to blame you, and I don't blame you. I may find fault with the system you administer, but pray understand that I know you are here to do a duty pointed out to you, and that I have no doubt you do it. Now, I hope you won't object to tell me what I want to know."

"No," said he, quite mollified, and very reasonable, "not at all. What is it?"

"Do you know that there are five wretched creatures outside?"

"I haven't seen them, but I dare say there are."

"Do you doubt that there are?"

"No, not at all. There might be many more."

"Are they men, or women?"

"Women, I suppose. Very likely one or two of them were there last night, and the night before last."

"There all night, do you mean?"

"Very likely."

My companion and I looked at one another, and the master of the Workhouse added quickly, "Why, Lord bless my soul! What am I to do? What can I do? The place is full. The place is always full—every night. I must give the preference to women with children, mustn't I? You wouldn't have me not do that?"

"Surely not," said I. "It is a very humane principle, and quite right; and I am glad to hear of it. Don't forget that I don't blame you."

"Well!" said he. And subdued himself again.

"What I want to ask you," I went on, "is whether you know any thing against those five miserable beings outside?"

"Don't know any thing about them," said he, with a wave of his arm.

"I ask, for this reason: that we mean to give them a trifle to get a lodging—if they are not shelterless because they are thieves, for instance. —You don't know them to be thieves?"

"I don't know anything about them," he repeated emphatically.

"That is to say, they are shut out, solely because the Ward is full?"

"Because the Ward is full."

"And if they got in, they would only have a roof for the night and a bit of bread in the morning, I suppose?"

"That's all. You'll use your own discretion about what you give them. Only understand that I don't know any thing about them beyond what I have told you."

"Just so. I wanted to know no more. You have answered my question civilly and readily, and I am much obliged to you. I have nothing to say against you, but quite the contrary. Good-night!"

"Good-night, gentlemen!" And out we came again.

We went to the ragged bundle nearest to the Workhouse-door, and I touched it. No movement replying, I gently shook it. The rags began to be slowly stirred within, and by little and little a head was unshrouded. The head of a young woman of three or four-and-twenty, as I should judge; gaunt with want, and foul with dirt, but not naturally ugly.

"Tell us," said I, stooping down, "why are you lying here?"

"Because I can't get into the Workhouse."

She spoke in a faint, dull way, and had no curiosity or interest left. She looked dreamily at the black sky and the falling rain, but never looked at me or my companion.

"Were you here last night?"

"Yes. All last night. And the night afore too."

"Do you know any of these others?"

"I know her next but one. She was here last night, and she told me she come out of Essex. I don't know no more of her."

"You were here all last night, but you have not been here all day?"

"No. Not all day."

"Where have you been all day?"

"About the streets."

"What have you had to eat?"

"Nothing."

"Come!" said I. "Think a little. You are tired and have been asleep, and don't quite consider what you are saying to us. You have had something to eat to-day. Come! Think of it!"

"No I haven't. Nothing but such bits as I could pick up about the market. Why, look at me!"

She bared her neck, and I covered it up again.

"If you had a shilling to get some supper and a lodging, should you know where to get it?"

"Yes. I could do that."

"For God's sake get it then!"

I put the money into her hand, and she feebly rose up and went away. She never thanked me, never looked at me—melted away into the miserable night, in the strangest manner I ever saw. I have seen many strange things, but not one that has left a deeper impression on my memory than the dull impassive way in which that worn-out heap of misery took that piece of money, and was lost.

One by one I spoke to all the five. In every one, interest and curiosity were as extinct as in the first. They were all dull and languid. No one made any sort of profession or complaint; no one cared to look at me; no one thanked me. When I came to the third, I suppose she saw that my companion and I glanced, with a new horror upon us, at the two last, who had dropped against each other in their sleep, and were lying like broken images. She said, she believed they were young sisters. These were the only words that were originated among the five.

And now let me close this terrible account with a redeeming and beautiful trait of the poorest of the poor. When we came out of the Workhouse, we had gone across the road to a public-house, finding ourselves without silver, to get change for a sovereign. I held the money in my hand while I was speaking to the five apparitions. Our being so engaged, attracted the attention of many people of the very poor sort usual to that place; as we leaned over the mounds of rags, they eagerly leaned over us to see and hear; what I had in my hand, and what I said, and what I did, must have been plain to nearly all the concourse. When the last of the five had got up and faded away, the spectators opened to let us pass; and not one of them, by word, or look, or gesture, begged of us. Many of the observant faces were quick enough to know that it would have been a relief to us to have got rid of the rest of the money with any hope of doing good with it. But there was a feeling among them all that their necessities were not to be placed by the side of such a spectacle; and they opened a way for us in profound silence, and let us go.

My companion wrote to me, next day, that the five ragged bundles had been upon his bed all night. I debated how to add our testimony to that of many other persons who from time to time are impelled to write to the newspapers, by having come upon some shameful and shocking sight of this description. I resolved to write an exact account of what we had seen, but to wait until after Christmas, in order that there might be no heat or haste. I know that the unreasonable disciples of a reasonable school, demented disciples who push arithmetic and political economy beyond all bounds of sense (not to speak of such a weakness as humanity), and hold them to be all-sufficient for every case, can easily prove that such things ought to be, and that no man has any business to mind them. Without disparaging those indispensable sciences in their sanity, I utterly renounce and abominate them in their insanity; and I address people with a respect for the spirit of the New Testament, who do mind such things, and who think them infamous in our streets.

"The American Forests"
By John Muir
1897

Born in Scotland on April 21, 1838, John Muir immigrated to America in 1849. His early years among the wilds of the Scottish highlands gave him a sense of the wonders and beauties that the natural world could provide. Later, he would attend the University of Wisconsin, and his early love of nature would drive him to study geology and botany.

Despite having to leave the university early to avoid the draft during the Civil War, Muir kept at his career as a naturalist. In 1867, he suffered an accident that temporarily blinded him. Upon recovering his sight, he embarked on a walking tour to the Amazon River Basin in South America. He recorded his thoughts on the natural world and landscape in a journal later published posthumously as A Thousand-Mile Walk to the Gulf. *It was in this journal that he would begin to develop his philosophy of how man and the natural world should interact with each other.* Muir's enlightening and inspiring ideals, in the face of industrialization, would place him as a giant in the American conservation movement of the early twentieth century.

Muir's various travels, especially in the Yosemite Valley of California, led him to advocate a system of national parks that would remain unspoiled and totally off-limits to development and economic exploitation. In 1890, he was successful in getting his beloved Yosemite Valley designated as a national park. In 1892, he and other like-minded people would form the Sierra Club, which even today remains as a beacon in the worldwide conservation movement.

The forests of America, however slighted by man, must have been a great delight to God; for they were the best he ever planted. The whole continent was a garden, and from the beginning it seemed to be favored above all the other wild parks and gardens of the globe. To prepare the ground, it was rolled and sifted in seas with infinite loving deliberation and forethought, lifted into the light, submerged and warmed over and over again, pressed and crumpled into folds and ridges, mountains and hills, subsoiled with heaving volcanic fires, ploughed and ground and sculptured into scenery and soil with glaciers and rivers,—every feature growing and changing from beauty to beauty, higher and higher. And in the fullness of time it was planted in groves, and belts, and broad, exuberant, mantling forests, with the largest, most varied, most fruitful, and most beautiful trees in the world. Bright seas made its border with wave embroidery and icebergs; gray deserts were outspread in the middle of it, mossy tundras on the north, savannas on the south, and blooming prairies and plains; while lakes and rivers shone through all the vast forests and openings, and happy birds and beasts gave delightful animation. Everywhere, everywhere over all the blessed continent, there were beauty, and melody, and kindly, wholesome, foodful abundance.

These forests were composed of about five hundred species of trees, all of them in some way useful to man, ranging in size from twenty-five feet in height and less than one foot in diameter at the ground to four hundred feet in height and more than twenty feet in diameter,—lordly monarchs proclaiming the gospel of beauty like apostles. For many a century after the ice-ploughs were melted, nature fed them and dressed them every day; working like a man, a loving, devoted, painstaking gardener; fingering every leaf and flower and mossy furrowed bole; bending, trimming, modeling, balancing, painting them with the loveliest colors; bringing over them now clouds with cooling shadows and showers, now sunshine; fanning them with gentle winds and rustling their leaves; exercising them in every fibre with storms, and pruning them; loading them with flowers and fruit, loading them with snow, and ever making them more beautiful as the years rolled by. Wide branching oak and elm in endless variety, walnut and maple, chestnut and beech, ilex and locust, touching limb to limb, spread a leafy translucent canopy along the coast of the Atlantic over the wrinkled folds and ridges of the Alleghenies,—a green billowy sea in summer, golden and purple in autumn, pearly gray like a steadfast frozen mist of interlacing branches and sprays in leafless, restful winter . . .

So they appeared a few centuries ago when they were rejoicing in wildness. The Indians with stone axes could do them no more harm than could gnawing beavers and browsing moose. Even the fires of the Indians and the fierce shattering lightning seemed to work together only for good in clearing spots here and there for smooth garden prairies, and openings for sunflowers seeking the light. But when the steel axe of the white man rang out in the startled air their doom was sealed. Every tree heard the bodeful sound, and pillars of smoke gave the sign in the sky.

I suppose we need not go mourning the buffaloes. In the nature of things they had to give place to better cattle, though the change might have been made without barbarous wickedness. Likewise many of nature's five hundred kinds of wild trees had to make way for orchards and cornfields. In the settlement and civilization of the country, bread more than timber or beauty was wanted; and in the blindness of hunger, the early settlers, claiming Heaven as their guide, regarded God's trees as only a larger kind of pernicious weeds, extremely hard to get rid of. Accordingly, with no eye to the future, these pious destroyers waged interminable forest wars; chips flew thick and fast; trees in their beauty fell crashing by millions, smashed to confusion, and the smoke of their burning has been rising to heaven more than two hundred years. After the Atlantic coast from Maine to Georgia had been mostly cleared and scorched into melancholy ruins, the overflowing multitude of bread and money seekers poured over the Alleghenies into the fertile middle West, spreading ruthless devastation ever wider and farther over the rich valley of the Mississippi and the vast shadowy pine region about the Great Lakes. Thence still westward the invading horde of destroyers called settlers made its fiery way over the broad Rocky Mountains, felling and burning more fiercely than ever, until at last it has reached the wild side of the continent, and entered the last of the great aboriginal forests on the shores of the Pacific.

Surely, then, it should not be wondered at that lovers of their country, bewailing its baldness, are now crying aloud, "Save what is left of the forests!" Clearing has surely now gone far enough; soon timber will be scarce, and not a grove will be left to rest in or pray in. The remnant protected will yield plenty of timber, a perennial harvest for every right use, without further diminution of its area, and will continue to cover the springs of the rivers that rise in the mountains and give irrigating water to the dry valleys at their feet, prevent wasting floods and be a blessing to everybody forever.

Every other civilized nation in the world has been compelled to care for its forests, and so must we if waste and destruction are not to go on to the bitter end, leaving America as barren as Palestine or Spain. In its calmer moments in the midst of bewildering hunger and war and restless over-industry, Prussia has learned that the forest plays an important part in human progress, and that the advance in civilization only makes it more indispensable. It has, therefore, as shown by Mr. [Gifford] Pinchot, refused to deliver its forests to more or less speedy destruction by permitting them to pass into private ownership. But the state woodlands are not allowed to lie idle. On the contrary, they are made to produce as much timber as is possible without spoiling them. In the administration of its forests, the state righteously considers itself bound to treat them as a trust for the nation as a whole, and to keep in view the common good of the people for all time . . .

It seems, therefore, that almost every civilized nation can give us a lesson on the management and care of forests. So far our government has done nothing effective with its forests, though the best in the world, but is like a rich and foolish spendthrift who has inherited a magnificent estate in perfect order, and then has left his rich fields and meadows, forests and parks, to be sold and plundered and wasted at will, depending on their inexhaustible abundance. Now it is plain that the forests are not inexhaustible, and that quick measures must be taken if ruin is to be avoided. Year by year the remnant is growing smaller before the axe and fire, while the laws in existence provide neither for the protection of the timber from destruction nor for its use where it is most needed . . .

The half dozen transcontinental railroad companies advertise the beauties of their lines in gorgeous many-colored folders, each claiming its as the "scenic route." "The route of superior desolation"—the smoke, dust, and ashes route— would be a more truthful description. Every train rolls on through dismal smoke and barbarous melancholy ruins; and the companies might well cry in their advertisements: "Come!

PRODUCTION, DISTRIBUTION, AND CONSUMPTION: THE IMPACT OF THE REVOLUTION

travel our way. Ours is the blackest. It is the only genuine Erebus route. The sky is black and the ground is black, and on either side there is a continuous border of black stumps and logs and blasted trees appealing to heaven for help as if still half alive, and their mute eloquence is most interestingly touching. The blackness is perfect. On account of the superior skill of our workmen, advantages of climate, and the kind of trees, the charring is generally deeper along our line, and the ashes are deeper, and the confusion and desolation displayed can never be rivaled. No other route on this continent so fully illustrates the abomination of desolation." Such a claim would be reasonable, as each seems the worst, whatever route you chance to take . . .

Notwithstanding all the waste and use which have been going on unchecked like a storm for more than two centuries, it is not yet too late, though it is high time, for the government to begin a rational administration of its forests. About seventy million acres it still owns,—enough for all the country, if wisely used. These residual forests are generally on mountain slopes, just where they are doing the most good, and where their removal would be followed by the greatest number of evils; the lands they cover are too rocky and high for agriculture, and can never be made as valuable for any other crop as for the present crop of trees. It has been shown over and over again that if these mountains were to be stripped of their trees and underbrush and kept bare and sodless by hordes of sheep and the innumerable fires the shepherds set, besides those of the millmen, prospectors, shake-makers, and all sorts of adventurers, both lowlands and mountains would speedily become little better than deserts, compared while their present beneficent fertility. During heavy rainfalls and while the winter accumulations of snow were melting, the larger streams would swell into destructive torrents; cutting deep, rugged-edged gullies, carrying away the fertile humus and soil as well as sand and rocks, filling up and overflowing their lower channels, and covering the lowland fields with raw detritus. Drought and barrenness would follow . . .

The United States government has always been proud of the welcome it has extended to good men of every nation, seeking freedom and homes and bread. Let them be welcomed still as nature welcomes them, to the woods as well as to the prairies and plains. No place is too good for good men, and still there is room. They are invited to heaven, and may well be allowed in America. Every place is made better by them. Let them be as free to pick gold and gems from the hills, to cut and hew, dig and plant, for homes and bread, as the birds are to pick berries from the wild bushes, and moss and leaves for nests. The ground will be glad to feed them, and the pines will come down from the mountains for their homes as willingly as the cedars came from Lebanon for Solomon's temple. Nor will the woods be the worse for this use, or their benign influences be diminished any more than the sun is diminished by shining. Mere destroyers, however, tree-killers, spreading death and confusion in the fairest groves and gardens ever planted, let the government hasten to cast them out and make an end of them. For it must be told again and again, and be burningly borne in mind, that just now, while protective measures are being deliberated languidly, destruction and use are speeding on faster and farther every day. The axe and saw are insanely busy, chips are flying thick as snowflakes, and every summer thousands of acres of priceless forests, with their underbrush, soil, springs, climate, scenery, and religion, are vanishing away in clouds of smoke, while, except in the national parks, not one forest guard is employed.

All sorts of local laws and regulations have been tried and found wanting, and the costly lessons of our own experience, as well as that of every civilized nation, show conclusively that the fate of the remnant of our forests is in the hands of the federal government, and that if the remnant is to be saved at all, it must be saved quickly.

Any fool can destroy trees. They cannot run away; and if they could, they would still be destroyed,—chased and hunted down as long as fun or a dollar could be got out of their bark hides, branching horns, or magnificent bole backbones. Few that fell trees plant them; nor would planting avail much towards getting back anything like the noble primeval forests. During a man's life only saplings can be grown, in the place of the old trees—tens of centuries old—that have been destroyed. It took more than three thousand years to make some of the trees in these Western woods,—trees that are still standing in perfect strength and beauty, waving and singing in the mighty forests of the Sierra. Through all the wonderful, eventful centuries since Christ's time—and long before that—God has cared for these trees, saved them from drought, disease, avalanches, and a thousand straining, leveling tempests and floods; but he cannot save them from fools,— only Uncle Sam can do that.

CHAPTER FIVE

POWER, AUTHORITY, AND GOVERNANCE: A NEW WORLD ORDER

Address at Minneapolis
President William McKinley
1899

As the twenty-fifth president of the United States, William McKinley guided the United States onto the course of imperialist expansion overseas. During the Cuban revolution against Spain, begun in 1896, he saw an opportunity to increase American power. Under McKinley's guidance, the United States supported the Cuban rebels, which ultimately led to the Spanish-American War of 1898.

After the war, the United States gained control of a vast swath of territories, including Puerto Rico in the Atlantic, and Guam, Hawaii, and the Philippines in the Pacific. Public sentiment on what to do with these new acquisitions, especially the Philippines, was very mixed. The president saw a moral duty to annex the Philippines and rule the islands in an authoritative fashion until the inhabitants were ready to govern themselves in a "civilized" manner. Others, including such prominent men as industrialist Andrew Carnegie and writers Mark Twain and

William James, believed that these policies would damage America's republican character. Furthermore, the Filipinos themselves had long been fighting for independence from Spain and did not welcome trading one ruling power for another. In February 1899, under the leadership of Emilio Aguinaldo, the Filipinos began a revolt to force the Americans out.

The speech below was delivered on October 12, 1899, while hostilities were still raging between Philippine guerrillas and American forces on the islands. In it, McKinley lays out the justifications for the annexation of the islands and the other imperial policies he had set out for the United States.

This century has been most memorable in the world's progress and history. The march of mankind in moral and intellectual advancement has been onward and upward. The growth of the world's material interests is so vast that the figures would almost seem to be drawn from the realm of imagination rather than from the field of fact. All peoples have felt the elevating influences of the century. Humanity and home have been lifted up. Nations have been drawn closer together in feeling and interest and sentiment. Contact has removed old prejudices at home and abroad, and brought about a better understanding, which has destroyed enmity and promoted amity. Civilization has achieved great victories, and to the gospel of good will there are now few dissenters. The great powers, under the inspiration of the Czar of Russia, have been sitting together in a parliament of peace, seeking to find a common basis for the adjustment of controversies without war and waste. While they have not made war impossible, they have made peace more probable, and have emphasized the universal love of peace. They have made a gain for the world's repose; and Americans, while rejoicing in what was accomplished, rejoice also for their participation in the great cause, yet to be advanced, we trust, to more perfect fulfillment.

The century has blessed us as a nation. While it has not given us perfect peace, it has brought us constant and ever-increasing blessings, and imposed upon us no humiliation or dishonor.

We have had wars with foreign powers, and the unhappy one at home; but all terminated in no loss of prestige or honor or territory, but a gain in all.

The increase of our territory has added vastly to our strength and prosperity without changing our republican character. It has given wider scope to democratic principles and enlarged the area for republican institutions.

I sometimes think we do not realize what we have, and the solemn trust we have committed to our keeping. The study of geography and history has now more than a passing interest to the American people. It is worth recalling that when the Federal Union was formed we held 909,050 square miles of territory, and in less than one hundred years we have grown to 3,845,694 square miles.

The first acquisition, in 1803, known as the Louisiana Purchase, embraced 883,072 square miles, exclusive of the area west of the Rocky Mountains. Its vastness and value will be best understood when I say that it comprises the entire States of Arkansas, Missouri, Iowa, Nebraska, North and South Dakota, and parts of the States of Minnesota, Kansas, Colorado, Montana, Wyoming, Louisiana, all of the Indian Territory, and part of Oklahoma Territory. It would seem almost incredible to the present generation that this rich addition to the federal domain should have been opposed; and yet it was resisted in every form and by every kind of assault. The ceded territory was characterized as a "malarial swamp," its prairies destitute of trees or vegetation. It was commonly charged that we had been cheated by giving fifteen million dollars for a territory so worthless and pestilential that it could never be inhabited or put to use; and it was also gravely asserted that the purchase would lead to complications and wars with European powers . . .

A distinguished representative from Virginia said he feared the effect of the vast extent of our empire; he feared the effects of the increased value of labor, the decrease in the value of lands, and the influence of climate upon our citizens who should migrate thither. He did fear (though this land was represented as flowing with milk and honey) that this Eden of the New World would prove a cemetery for the bodies of our citizens who emigrated to it.

Imperialism, as it was termed, had a chief place in the catalogue of disasters which would follow the ratification of the Louisiana treaty, and it was alleged that this was the first and sure step to the creation of an empire and the subversion of the Constitution. The expression "planetary policy," which is now employed by some critics, so far as I have been able to discover, first appeared here. Jefferson was made the subject of satirical verse:

See him commence, land speculator, And buy up the realm of nature, Towns, cities, Indians, Spaniards, prairies . . .

The opponents, however, were in the minority, and the star of the republic did not set, and the mighty West was brought under the flag of justice, freedom, and opportunity. In 1819 we added 69,749 square miles, which now comprise Florida and parts of Alabama, Mississippi, and Louisiana.

In 1845 we received the cession of Texas. It contained 376,931 square miles, and embraced the State of Texas and parts of Oklahoma, Kansas, Colorado, Wyoming, and New Mexico.

The next cession was under the treaty of 1848, containing 522,568 square miles, embracing the States of California, Nevada, Utah, and parts of Colorado and Wyoming, and of the Territories of Arizona and New Mexico.

In 1853 we acquired by the Gadsden Purchase 45,535 square miles, which embrace parts of Arizona and New Mexico.

The next great acquisition was that of Alaska in 1867, containing 599,446 square miles. This treaty, like that for the Louisiana Purchase, was fiercely resisted. When the House had under consideration the bill appropriating the sum of $7,200,000, the amount of purchase-money for Alaska agreed upon by the treaty, the minority report on that bill quoted approvingly an article which characterized Alaska as a "terra incognita," and stated "that persons well informed as to Alaska are ungrateful enough to hint that we could have bought a much superior elephant in Siam or Bombay for one hundredth part of the money, with not a ten thousandth part of the expense incurred in keeping the animal in proper condition."

The minority report proceeded to say that

The committee, having considered the various questions involved and the evidence in regard to this country under consideration, is forced to the conclusion that the possession of the country is of no value to the government of the United States. That it will be a source of weakness instead of power, and a constant annual expense for which there will be no adequate return. That it has no capacity as an agricultural country. That so far as known it has no value as a mineral country . . . That its fur trade is of insignificant value to us as a nation, and will speedily come to an end. That the fisheries are of doubtful value, and that whatever the value of its fisheries, its fur trade, its timber, or its minerals, they were all open to the citizens of the United States under existing treaties. That the right to govern a nation or nations of savages, in a climate unfit for the habitation of civilized men, was not worthy of purchase . . . They therefore report the following resolution: Resolved, That it is inexpedient to appropriate money for the purchase of Russian America.

In the debate in the House a distinguished representative from Massachusetts said:

If we are to pay for Russia's friendship this amount, I desire to give her the $7,200,000 and let her keep Alaska. I have no doubt that at any time within the last twenty years we could *have had Alaska for the asking, provided we would have taken it as a gift; but no man, except one insane enough to buy the earthquakes of St. Thomas and the ice-fields of Greenland, could be found to agree to any other terms for its acquisition to this country.*

To this treaty the opponents were in the minority; and that great, rich territory, from which we have drawn many and many times over its purchase price, and with phenomenal wealth yet undeveloped, is ours in spite of their opposition.

In the last year we have added to the territory belonging to the United States the Hawaiian Islands, one of the gems of the Pacific Ocean, containing 6740 square miles; Porto Rico, containing 3600 square miles; Guam, containing 175 square miles; and the Philippine archipelago, embracing approximately 143,000 square miles. This latest acquisition is about one sixth the size of the original thirteen States. It is larger than the combined area of New Jersey, Delaware, Maryland, Virginia, North Carolina, South Carolina, and the District of Columbia. It exceeds in area all of the New England States. It is almost as large as Washington and Oregon combined, and greater than Ohio, Indiana, and Illinois united; three times larger than New York, and three and one half times larger than the State of Ohio.

The treaty of peace with Spain, which gave us the Philippines, Porto Rico, and Guam, met with some opposition in the Senate, but was ratified by that body by more than a two thirds vote; while in the House the appropriation of twenty million dollars was made with little or no opposition. As in the case of the Louisiana Purchase and Alaska, the opponents of the treaty were in the minority, and the star of hope to an oppressed people was not extinguished. The future of these new possessions is in the keeping of Congress, and Congress is the servant of the people. That they will be retained under the benign sovereignty of the United States I do not permit myself to doubt. That they will prove a rich and invaluable heritage I feel assured. That Congress will provide for them a government which will bring them blessings, which will promote their material interests as well as advance their people in the path of civilization and intelligence, I confidently believe. They will not be governed as vassals or serfs or slaves; they will be given a government of liberty, regulated by law, honestly administered, without oppressing exactions, taxation without tyranny, justice without bribe, education without distinction of social condition, freedom of religious worship, and protection in "life, liberty, and the pursuit of happiness."

"Aguinaldo's Case Against the United States"
By a Filipino
1899

Emilio Aguinaldo was a leader of the Filipino independence movement at the turn of the twentieth century. He joined the Katipunan, a secret revolutionary group founded by Andres Bonifacio, in March 1895 and quickly rose to prominence. In the next two years, he would play a major role in trying to push the Spanish out of the Philippines, going so far as to declare a republic of the Philippines in

1897 and getting himself elected its president, though by December of that year he was forced to go into exile in Hong Kong.

The Spanish-American War began in April of the following year, and on May 1, 1898, Admiral George Dewey defeated the Spanish fleet moored in Manila Bay. Aguinaldo returned to Manila on May 18, with the backing of the United States, to lead a Filipino revolt against the Spanish, with the understanding that should they win, the Philippines would have independence.

However, President McKinley believed that possession of the Philippines was vital to U.S. interests in the Pacific, and after the Spanish surrendered to Admiral Dewey on August 18, 1898, control of the country passed into the hands of an American military governor. After the Treaty of Peace was signed between the United States and Spain, President McKinley issued his Benevolent Assimilation Proclamation, which declared the Philippines to be United States territory. This sparked Aguinaldo to call for a new guerrilla campaign to win independence from the United States.

Issued by an anonymous representative of Aguinaldo's revolutionary government of the Republic of the Philippines, the following essay lays out the Filipino case for independence. Hoping to sway American public opinion, the author appeals to his American audience's memory of its own country's revolutionary past.

———□———

A short time ago, the American people were painfully shocked into a sense of the truth as to the condition of affairs in the Philippine Islands, by the protests of the newspaper correspondents that [Brigadier-general H. G.] Otis was deliberately falsifying the reports of the Philippine campaign to suit public vanity. This by means of a rigid censorship, instituted by his "sovereign" commands, he has done in the most efficacious manner, and the American people awoke the other day, not, like the English poet Byron, to find themselves famous, but to realize the fact that they have been miserably duped. The resignation or demission of Secretary [Russell] Alger was a necessary consequence of this revelation.

We Filipinos have all along believed that if the American nation at large knew exactly, as we do, what is daily happening in the Philippine Islands, they would rise *en masse,* and demand that this barbaric war should stop. There are other methods of securing sovereignty—the true and lasting sovereignty that has its foundation in the hearts of the people. Has not the greatest of English poets said:

> *"Kind hearts are more than coronets,*
> *And simple faith than Norman blood?"*

And, did America recognize this fact, she would cease to be the laughing stock of other civilized nations, as she became when she abandoned her traditions and set up a double standard of government—government by consent in America, government by force in the Philippine Islands.

"Coming events cast their shadows before." Let us look at the situation exactly as it is, as we know it to be, and let the American people no longer deceive themselves or be deceived by others.

Politically speaking, we know that we are simply regarded as the means to an end. For the time being, we are crushed under the wheels of the modern political Juggernaut, but its wheels are not broad enough to crush us all. Perfidious Albion is the prime mover in this dastardly business—she at one side of the lever, America at the other, and the fulcrum in the Philippines. England has set her heart on the Anglo-American alliance. She is using America as a cat's-paw. What she cannot obtain by force, she intends to secure by stratagem. Unknown to the great majority of the American people, she has taken the American government into her confidence, and shown it "the glorious possibilities of the East." The temptation has proved too strong. Now, in this, England is playing a double game, on the principle of "heads I win, tails you lose." If America should win, all is well; England has her ally safely installed in the East, ready at her beck and call to oppose, hand in hand with her, the other powers in the dismemberment of the Orient. If America loses, she will be all the more solicitous to join in the Anglo-American alliance. The other powers stand by and see this political combination effected, while their plenipotentiaries gravely discuss, at the Hague, the theoretical aspects of universal peace, and are deaf to the wail of the widows and the orphans, and to the cry of an oppressed race struggling to be free. Such is "man's inhumanity to man."

You have been deceived all along the line. You have been greatly deceived in the personality of my countrymen. You went to the Philippines under the impression that their inhabitants were ignorant savages, whom Spain had kept in subjection at the bayonet's point. The Filipinos have been described in serious American journals as akin to the hordes of the Khalifa; and the idea has prevailed that it required only some unknown American Kitchener to march triumphantly from north to south to make the military occupation complete. We have been represented by your popular press as if we were Africans or Mohawk Indians. We smile, and deplore the want of ethnological knowledge on the part of our literary friends. We are none of these. We are simply Filipinos. You know us now in part: you will know us better, I hope, by and by.

Some clear-headed men in the United States Senate knew the facts; but, alas, genius and correct thinking are ever in the minority.

I will not deny that there are savages in the Philippine Islands, if you designate by that name those who lead a nomad life, who do not pay tribute or acknowledge sovereignty to any one save their chief. For, let it be remembered, Spain held these islands for three hundred years, but never conquered more than one-quarter of them, and that only superficially and chiefly by means of priest-craft. The Spaniards never professed to derive their just powers from the consent of those whom they attempted to govern. What they took by force, they lost by force at our hands; and you deceived yourselves when you bought a revolution for twenty million dollars, and entangled yourselves in international politics. "Non decipimur specie recti?" [Latin: We are deceived by your show of righteousness.] You imagined you had bought the Philippines and the Filipinos for this mess of pottage. Your imperialism led you, blind-fold, to purchase "sovereignty" from a third party who had no title to give you—a confidence trick, certainly, very transparent; a bad bargain, and one we have had sufficient perspicuity and education to see through.

In the struggle for liberty which we have ever waged, the education of the masses has been slow; but we are not, on that account, an uneducated people, as our records show. Your Senators, even, admit that our political documents are worthy of a place in the archives of any civilized nation. It is the fittest and the best of our race who have survived the vile oppression of the Spanish Government, on the one hand, and of their priests on the other; and, had it not been for their tyrannous "sovereignty" and their execrable colonial methods, we would have been, ere this time, a power in the East, as our neighbors, the Japanese, have become by their industry and their modern educational methods.

You repeat constantly the dictum that we cannot govern ourselves. [English historian and politician Thomas Babington] Macaulay long ago exposed the fallacy of this statement as regards colonies in general. With equal reason, you might have said the same thing some fifty or sixty years ago of Japan; and, little over a hundred years ago, it was extremely questionable, when you, also, were rebels against the English Government, if you could govern yourselves. You obtained the opportunity, thanks to political combinations and generous assistance at the critical moment. You passed with credit through the trying period when you had to make a beginning of governing yourselves, and you eventually succeeded in establishing a government on a republican basis, which, theoretically, is as good a system of government as needs be, as it fulfils the just ideals and aspirations of the human race.

Now, the moral of all this obviously is: Give us the chance; treat us exactly as you demanded to be treated at the hands of England, when you rebelled against her autocratic methods. Deal only with facts in a rational and consistent way. Leave empiricism alone, and address yourselves seriously to the work of seeking the solution that shall be honorable to both parties. We know all the wire-pullers who are at work. We can tell you far more than you know; for we know our country and our countrymen, their past history, and what is necessary for their future good.

Now, here is an unique spectacle—the Filipinos fighting for liberty, the American people fighting them to give them liberty. The two peoples are fighting on parallel lines for the same object. We know that parallel lines never meet. Let us look back to discover the point at which the lines separated and the causes of the separation, so that we may estimate the possibility of one or the other or both being turned inwards so that they shall meet again.

You declared war with Spain for the sake of Humanity. You announced to the world that your programme was to set Cuba free, in conformity with your constitutional principles. One of your ablest officials gave it as his opinion that the Filipinos were far more competent to govern themselves than the Cuban people were.

You entered into an alliance with our chiefs at Hong Kong and at Singapore, and you promised us your aid and protection in our attempt to form a government on the principles and after the model of the government of the United States. Thereupon you sent a powerful fleet to Manila and demolished the old

Spanish hulks, striking terror into the hearts of the Spanish garrison in Manila. In combination with our forces, you compelled Spain to surrender, and you proclaimed that you held the city, port and bay of Manila until such time as you should determine what you meant by the word "control," as applied to the rest of the islands. By some mysterious process, heretofore unknown to civilized nations, you resolved "control" into "sovereignty," on the pretense that what is paid for is "possession," no matter what the quality of the title may be . . .

The rest is a matter of history, of which the American public, otherwise lamentably ignorant of details, possess at least Gen. Otis' version, which, needless to say, is far from being the correct one. The administration defend themselves by saying that they know the truth. The more shame to them that they continue this barbarous and unjust warfare!

You have been deceived from the beginning, and deception is the order of the day. You continue to deceive yourselves by the thought that once the military power is established in the Philippines, the rest is a matter for politicians. Verily you are falling into the pit you have dug for yourselves. Your officials and generals have broken their promises with our countrymen over and over again. Your atrocious cruelties are equalled only by those of Spain.

You take into your confidence the odious reptiles of Spanish priestcraft. You have established a reputation for the historical Punica Fides. In the face of the world you emblazon Humanity and Liberty upon your standard, while you cast your political constitution to the winds and attempt to trample down and exterminate a brave people whose only crime is that they are fighting for their liberty. You ask my countrymen to believe in you, to trust you, and you assure them that, if they do so, all will be well. But your action is on a plane with the trick which the vulgar charlatan at a country fair plays upon the unwary with three cards and an empty box.

You will never conquer the Philippine Islands by force alone. How many soldiers in excess of the regular army do you mean to leave in every town, in every province? How many will the climate claim as its victims, apart from those who may fall in actual warfare? What do the American people, who have thousands of acres yet untilled, want with the Philippines? Have you figured up the cost? . . .

The man, next to Gen. [Wesley] Merritt, who has misled you, and who is responsible for the continuance of this barbarous warfare, is General Otis. Had he allowed the Peace Commission to act independently, a modus vivendi [a method of living] would probably have been arrived at. But this question of sovereignty—why, such a transparent farce has never before been flouted before an intelligent people and the world in general. Can you wonder our people mistrust you and your empirical methods? They do not even regard you as being serious—a nation which professes to derive its just power of government from the consent of the governed.

"Lay down your arms," you say. Did you lay down your arms when you, too, were rebels, and the English under good King George demanded your submission? How in the name of all that is serious do you demand that we shall do what you, being rebels, refused to do?

Therefore, we Filipinos say: "Recall Gen. Otis, give the Peace Commission a free hand, try rather methods of fair dealing, make our countrymen believe that you are sincere, and be sincere and just in your dealings with them. Suspend the order for these rabble volunteers, the scum of your country, whom you propose to send across the sea to die of the effect of the climate, and you will find you can do more in a month than you will do by force in twenty years. Your scheme of military occupation has been a miserable failure. You have gained practically nothing. With General Otis, or without him, you will have to commence at the beginning again. Our forces are manufacturing thousands of cartridges and other improved means to continue the struggle, and it will continue until you are convinced of your error."

Our friend, Admiral Dewey, will undoubtedly have something to say to your President when he reaches home. He caught the genius of the Philippine people, and if he had been left alone many valuable lives would have been spared and many millions of treasure saved. Be convinced, the Philippines are for the Filipinos. We are a virile race. We have never assimilated with our former oppressors, and we are not likely to assimilate with you.

Negros and Cebu are wavering in the balance uncertain whether or not to continue under your jurisdiction. We know how all that came to pass and the intrigues in Manila. Your newspaper correspondents know it also. But I am violating the commands of Gen. Otis by letting you into the secret. Meanwhile, I subscribe myself

—*Semper Vigilans [Always vigilant]*

Reports of the War
By Stephen Crane
1898

Stephen Crane was not only a successful novelist and short story writer, but also an effective war correspondent, first covering the fighting between Greece and the Ottoman Empire, and then covering the Spanish-American War. His career was still blooming when he unfortunately contracted tuberculosis and died in 1900 at the age of twenty-nine.

Scholars often credit him as the first modern American writer, as his style was based on realistic depictions of events and settings. Published when he was just twenty-four, The Red Badge of Courage, *a story of a young soldier's experiences during the Civil War, is arguably his most famous book. Despite never having been in or seen combat, Crane managed to capture the horror and mind-set of a soldier facing and overcoming his fears while on the battlefield. It was this skill at crafting vivid and realistic descriptions of combat and the mind-set of the young soldiers who fought that later made him so effective as a war correspondent.*

Filing his work for such papers as Joseph Pulitzer's New York World *during the Spanish-American War, Crane chronicled such events as the landing of American troops at Guantanamo Bay, Cuba, and the charge up San Juan Hill. His tone in many of his dispatches, as shown in the following excerpt, is that of respect for the soldiers doing a dangerous job in a cause that is just. Crane's piece explores the effects of colonialism, where any nation will eventually reflect the culture of the colonial power.*

PONCE, Porto Rico, Aug. 7.—As one of the Journal dispatch boats circled slowly past the war ships and transports into the harbor of Ponce the correspondents, veterans of Santiago, and other campaigns, began to array themselves disreputably. They donned breeches of brown duck and shirts of the hues of almost every kind of vegetable, and their hats were slouch, dirty, twisty-wise and a discredit to them. The correspondents also armed themselves. In the end they somewhat resembled jail birds, which is the business of men good at the game of war.

    The yacht dropped anchor and another correspondent came from the shore. He had arrived two days previously. Upon sighting the formidable group on the quarterdeck he burst into hoarse laughter. Later he explained the wonders of Ponce. It was no Daiquiri. It was no Siboney. It was no cable station at Guantanamo. Ponce, to be sure, was a city with hotels and shops and public hacks and barbers and ice and ales, wines, liquors and cigars. If a man lost all his lead pencils he could jaunt casually into the street and buy more. If there happened an unhappy soul with no tobacco, there was no period of intolerable anguish. In case of need, for instance, there could be found such a person as a dentist. And the correspondent went on to say that the generals and the newspaper men were in the habit of riding to the front—the terrible front—in carriages. The ferocity died out of the arriving war correspondents. In carriages? Name of heaven!

    Viewed ashore, Ponce, two miles from its little sea port, developed four striking things immediately—American buggies, naked babies, trees laden with flaming crimson blossoms, and the enigmatic smile of the Porto Rican. They were all burning in the sunshine and dimmed by the white dust of a tropic city. They were all guarded by the American soldier, a calm, bronze and blue man with a bayonet. And herein lay the supreme interest, the interest of the juxtaposition of Michigan and Porto Rico—Grand Rapids serenely sitting in judgment upon the affairs of Ponce. This made one marvel; this was the extraordinary situation that dazed the thoughtful American. It was as if a journal had announced: "A Rochester trolley car has collided with an ox cart in Buenos Ayres." You could not gauge the thing; you remained simply astounded.

Afterward there was the enigmatic smile of the Porto Rican. It was enigmatic at first because we thought of it too hard. We weighed it too much. We reflected upon it until it became simply confusion—a conciliatory, joyful, fearful, crafty, honest, lying smile. But at length emerged this fact—the Porto Rican, taking him as a symbolized figure, a type, was glad, glad that the Spaniards had gone, glad that the Americans had come. What the troops received at Ponce was a welcome. The cheering was led by the responsible men, the merchants, the land owners, the people with purses. When your man with a purse cheers he has got to mean it. Otherwise he would choke to death.

In the applause there is a stratum of deceit, but it is furnished mainly by the peasantry, who have been forcibly taught that the Spaniards are invincible and are sure to return. Meanwhile the American soldier expresses his opinion of this probability in a new word—Spinachers. The Jamaica negro cannot say Spaniard. His comic tongue makes him say Spuniard. The American soldier says Spinacher because when a thing becomes common he is nationally bound to extract from it whatever it may convey of our kind of irony.

Ponce, of course, bears the stamp of Spain, that stamp which shall remain forever upon Mexico and the States of Central America and South America, even as they are indelible in Cuba. It is a thing which cannot be conquered even by such superb troops as United States regulars. You can shoot a man through the head, but you cannot remove from his brain a love for the bloody death of a bull. There is the inevitable little plaza in the centre of the city, shaded with beautiful trees and threaded with wide walks. In the Moorish band stand a Spanish band operated but yesterday. Sometimes now an American band plays there of an evening. In the plaza there is also the cathedral, a fine old Spanish sign, such as one sees even in California. From the plaza radiate such streets and such scenes as one can find in the City of Mexico, the only thing lacking being the persistent, harsh cries of the street vendors. The principal hotel is the usual, quaint place, with a courtyard in which men sit and have their cognac or coffee. The walls are decorated with lamentable pictures in oil—fat and shapeless lions, palm trees, absurd urns, white palaces, lakes. The tropic sun blisters the paint, and pieces of lion, tree, palace have fallen to the ground. Dilapidation is carefully prominent here as in all the city. Every door, every window is as high as aspiration and almost as dingy as fulfillment. The Spaniard, when he is once persuaded to polish, is a terrible person. He creates a newness a thousand times more ghastly than his ordinary dirtiness. A clean and newly painted house in a Spanish town is unreal and terrifying. And so the old city lies in the sun, dirty, romantic and patrolled by Wisconsin.

CHAPTER SIX

CULTURE: THE LEGACY OF THE REVOLUTION

"Mass Production Makes a Better World"
By Edward A. Filene
1929

The Industrial Revolution changed not only the way people worked, but also the way the growing American populace consumed goods and services. As factories began to produce more and more different types of goods and products at prices that hand-crafted items could not match, a growing concern was to prevent over-production. One way to combat this phenomenon was to find a way to convince the swelling mass of consumers that not only could they afford these products but that they could not do without them.

A development that brought about this change in American consumption was the creation of the department store. These new, huge shopping emporiums were located in the hearts of rapidly growing cities. Combining an element of show business, by the use of huge window displays and extravagant architectural detailing, with innovations in merchandising such as charging fixed prices (kept as low as *possible to increase the total volume of sales), department stores helped create America's consumer culture—a direct result of the Industrial Revolution.*

A pioneer in the creation of the department store was the Filene family in Boston. The family's success was greatly due to its ability to create an environment that lured customers in, which included treating their sales force in a dignified and humane manner so that it would provide excellent customer service. The company's president, Edward Filene, believed that if he paid his workers enough, they would become the consumers that were needed to prevent the overproduction that would cause the system to collapse.

———◻———

It is agreed by competent observers in this country and in Europe that America's increasing general prosperity and high standards of living are due chiefly to the rapidly increasing use of scientific mass production and distribution.

Yet there are some—mostly impractical theorists—who profess to see in mass methods the threat of grave danger to mankind. Where I see good, they see evil. Where I see the means of liberating the masses of the people economically, the critics of mass methods see the probability that men will become veritable slaves of their machines. The theorists foretell an era of machine-made ugliness, while I look to low-cost mass production to make beauty more general and to put more of it within the reach of the masses. In short, the theorists assert that mass production and distribution are bad in many ways for both producers and consumers. I am convinced that they benefit both.

I am going to consider categorically the principal allegations which are made against mass methods. But first let us see clearly just what mass methods are and what they imply.

Scientific mass production, for example, is not merely the production of large quantities of highly standardized goods. It implies that those goods shall be made under the most modern and efficient methods, largely by means of machinery, and with a high degree of division, or specialization, of labor. The original aim was cost reduction rather than the production of great quantities of goods, but it was soon discovered that costs can be reduced to the minimum only by producing in large quantities—millions of articles—and thereby reducing "overhead" expense to the point where the charge against each unit is comparatively negligible.

But mass producers also found out that when goods are produced in great quantities there must be millions of consumers. It would be foolish, for instance, to make a million automobiles or two million pairs of shoes if you were going to charge $25,000 for each automobile and $50 for each pair of shoes.

Fortunately, mass production can produce consumers by creating buying power. This it does through (a) paying high wages; (b) selling cheaply. Because production per man is high, it is possible to pay high wages. Furthermore, when many articles are made by each worker under scientific mass methods the difference between a high wage and a low wage is a relatively small part of the cost of each article. Then mass producers discover that the greatest total profits are made from the smallest practical profit per unit, because only by selling cheaply can the price be brought within the reach of the masses of consumers.

However, merely to produce goods and to supply the buying power are seldom enough except for the most essential necessities of life. People will not usually buy, even when they have the necessary buying power, unless they want the goods. Therefore it is necessary that the goods made by mass-production methods be attractive in appearance and of good quality, if they are to be bought again and again . . .

It is obvious, with a little thought, that the masses of the American people are consuming many things which they could not afford to buy even ten years ago. The contribution of mass methods is reflected in the general comparatively high standard of living, in the rarity of acute poverty among those who are able and willing to work, and in the general ownership of such luxuries as the motor car and the wide use of the telephone.

The point is this: Mass production, by reducing costs and prices and by increasing wages, has increased the purchasing power of everyone. The increase in per capita consumption has kept pace with the increase in per capita production, so that, in the long run, mass production has not resulted in unemployment. The reverse is true.

Take the automobile industry as an example. In 1895 only four automobiles were made in the United States. Probably only a few dozen workmen were employed in the industry. For the next few years the increase in the use of cars was slow, chiefly because the price was high. Automobiles were rich men's toys. But, as mass production brought the price of cars down to a point where most people could afford to buy them, the sales of cars rapidly increased.

In fifteen years the production of cars per man hour increased tenfold. That is, in a given period one man can turn out the number of cars that ten men made fifteen years ago. To the old school of thought it would follow that nine men out of every ten were laid off in the automobile industry because of the improved methods. The fact is that the number of workers in the automobile and subsidiary industries has grown constantly until in 1926 there were employed, directly and indirectly, 3,743,781, according to figures of the National Automobile Chamber of Commerce. In 1919, in automobile and truck factories alone 210,559 workers were employed. In 1926 this figure had grown to 375,281, in spite of the fact that production per man hour had increased more than 25 per cent between 1919 and 1926.

While only 375,281 workers were employed in automobile and truck factories in 1926, hundreds of thousands more found employment in industries directly dependent on motor cars and trucks. For example, there were 320,000 workers in automobile-accessory factories; 100,000 tire-factory workers; 455,000 dealers and salesmen distributing automobiles, trucks, tires, and other accessories; 1,400,000 chauffeurs and truck drivers; 575,000 garage and repair-shop employees. The automobile is the largest consumer of gasoline and oils, and it is estimated that 110,000 workers in this field owe their employment to the motor industry . . .

So much for the objections made to mass production by those theorists who see in it an influence making for human unhappiness, dull uniformity, and ugliness. They are the ones who commonly have no first-hand knowledge of what mass production really is, of how it works, or of its true economic significance. It is perhaps not so very strange that those people should think they see a danger in a technique which they do not understand.

But it is truly strange that some business men, who certainly ought thoroughly to understand the full implications and methods of mass production, should see in it a danger to business as a whole. They hold that to sell the vast quantities of goods which mass methods produce calls for high-pressure and very expensive selling efforts which largely offset the economies made in the factory.

It is obvious that those who hold that view do not yet grasp all of the implications of mass production. They assume that we must have thrust down our throats the goods which mass production turns out. The fact is that there is still a tremendous potential, but ineffective, demand for large quantities of nearly every kind of goods. The reason why this potential demand does not manifest itself in effective demand, in actual consumption, is that the people have not yet the buying power they must have before they can satisfy all of their wants. Either they have insufficient wages, or the prices they are asked to pay are too high, or both.

As I have said, it is the part of mass production to increase their wages and to reduce the prices of the things the masses would like to buy but as yet cannot buy. When that is done, the potential demand will at once become effective, and those products which almost all people want will all but sell themselves. Expensive high-pressure methods are not necessary in order to sell wanted goods to people who have sufficient money with which to buy them. Producers must, of course, make sure that the commodities which they turn out in large volume are the things which large numbers of people want. The goods must fill a need, and be of proper quality and style.

It all comes down to this: Business, to succeed largely in these days, must produce in large quantities, pay high wages, and sell cheaply. That is the basis of prosperity—the buying power of the masses, which has been created by scientific mass methods in production and distribution. As prosperity spreads throughout the world it will become a bulwark against war. Contrary to a popular belief, peace is a growth, not a manufacture; which simply means that you cannot "make" a lasting peace.

Such a peace will be brought about only by conditions that are just to all—just to the rich as well as the poor. Above all, conditions that give every man the certainty of always getting enough work to earn an adequate living for his wife, his children, and himself; and to keep him and his fellow men from supporting war or revolution in the belief that any change is preferable to existing conditions.

Prosperity is the Road to Peace. Because of my deep conviction that this is true, I have joined with others in maintaining at Geneva the International Management Institute, which seeks to spread the knowledge and use of scientific mass methods in European industry. Mass methods will make Europe prosperous—as they have made America prosperous.

I have studied mass production in all of its aspects since its inception, and have watched its development. I have studied especially closely its social and economic aspects, and I can say without qualification that if it is used by leaders who understand that in order to make the greatest total profits they must pay ever-higher wages, constantly reduce prices, and keep profits per unit of output down to the very minimum, mass production holds no dangers to the common welfare, but on the contrary holds possibilities of accomplishing for mankind all of the good that theoretical reformers or irrational radicals hope to secure by revolutionary means.

"The Ideas of Progress"
From A Century of Progress
By Charles A. Beard
1933

Another outcome of the Industrial Revolution was its reinforcement of the idea that progress was the natural order of history. Many leading intellectuals addressed this idea in an attempt to show how the rapid expansion of material output had led to all sorts of benefits for American society. The idea that increasing technological and scientific sophistication led to better living standards due to better nutrition, health care, and social organization, was a constant theme of intellectuals' writings during this period, and in fact remains a central focal point in the American cultural landscape.

Charles A. Beard was a leading historian of American politics and economics in the early 1920s and 1930s. He was one of the first American historians to relate how economic interests affected political interest during the American Revolution, and this led him to broaden his study to the role economics played in politics in general. In the following selection, Beard lays out his argument that as a historical force, progress has been the most influential in the development of a modern Western civilization based on democratic ideals.

———◻———

Although hailed in some circles of conceit as a glorious symbol of more speed and bigger machines, and in others as a covering for cruel materialism, the concept of progress is one of the most profound and germinal ideas at work in the modern age. It is at the same time an interpretation of the long history of mankind and a philosophy of action in this world of bewildering choices. It gives a clue of meaning to the rise of civilization out of the crudities of primitive barbarism and offers a guide to the immense impending future. Briefly defined, it implies that mankind, by making use of science and invention, can progressively emancipate itself from plagues, famines, and social disasters, and subjugate the materials and forces of the earth to the purposes of the good life—here and now. In essence the idea of progress belongs to our own times, for it was unknown to the ancients and to the thinkers of the Middle Ages. It is associated, therefore, with every phase of the vast intellectual, economic, and rational movement which has transformed the classical and medieval heritage into what is called, for the sake of convenience, Western civilization.

Hence it is closely affiliated with democracy, natural science, technology, and social amelioration, and shares with them the strength of universality. It is more than a theory. It has achievements to its credit on every hand—diseases stamped out, pain silenced or assuaged, the span of life lengthened, famine made obsolete, comforts and conveniences established, sanitation supplied to multitudes, knowledge made popular through amazing instrumentalities of transmission and reproduction. And it suggests a faith of power, faith that the world, as [essayist and poet Ralph Waldo] Emerson said, "is all gates, all opportunities, strings of tension to be struck." Rejecting resignation as a philosophy of life, it confronts obstacles with assurance. Where the pessimist sees the worst, it proposes a search for the best and advances toward perfection by increments. The suffering, ignorance, and folly which drive the timid to the Nirvana of doubt and oblivion are, under the light of progress, calls to action, to research, to planning, and to conquest. Touched by the genius of universal emancipation, the idea cuts across the barriers of caste, class, race, and nationality, breaks through rigid boundaries, and regards the substances and forces of nature as potential instruments of humane purposes. Everywhere it makes its way, dissolving the feudal institutions of Europe, disturbing the slumbers of the Orient, arousing lethargic Russia, and finding a naked avowal in the United States of America: the earth may be subdued for the security, welfare, and delight of them that dwell therein . . .

During these momentous years, while the idea of progress was taking form, spreading, branching, and working its way into the remotest divisions of European thought, the English colonies in America grew to maturity and burst upon the world stage as a united and independent power. Here the

CULTURE: THE LEGACY OF THE REVOLUTION

natural resources, intellectual climate, and social order were highly favorable to the growth of the new concept. Here nature had provided an enormous and diversified material endowment which could be used to establish a high level of life and sustain the continuous advancement of standards, if intelligently and efficiently used. Here the population was ready for secular enterprise. While many had migrated to America in search of religious freedom, the great majority who came voluntarily had come for mundane reasons—the improvement of their condition here and now—and even those who fled for religious reasons expected, as a rule, to find a decent living somehow. All the factors which had contributed to the germination of the idea of progress in Europe were even more prominent in America—respect for industry and labor, a preoccupation with secular enterprise, and a spirit of experimentation and invention.

In these circumstances, the leading thinkers of the New World, especially [Benjamin] Franklin and [Thomas] Paine, carried the idea of progress more or less consciously into the plans they formulated for American culture. "It is impossible to imagine," wrote the former, "the height to which may be carried, in a thousand years, the power of man over matter. We may perhaps learn to deprive large masses of their gravity and give them levity, for the sake of easy transportation. Agriculture may diminish its labor and double its produce; all diseases may by sure means be prevented or cured, not excepting that of old age, and our lives lengthened at pleasure even beyond the antediluvian standard. O that moral science were in a fair way of improvement, that men would cease to be wolves to one another and that human beings would at length learn what they now improperly call humanity!" Thomas Paine, in his *Rights of Man*, written in answer to Edmund Burke's *Reflections on the French Revolution*—a plea for historic conservatism—sketched an outline of political economy that embraced universal education, the abolition of poverty, reform of the criminal law, pensions for the aged, the reduction of armaments, and international peace . . .

With inescapable fatality the mass production made possible by machinery and nourished by our unparalleled natural resources accelerated the leveling democracy implied in the idea of progress. Gigantic industries could not flourish without an immense market. And where was that market to be found? In a small privileged class enriched by the profits of capitalism? Only one answer was possible. The few craftsmen of the Middle Ages might sell the choice products of loom, forge, kiln, and chisel to lords, ladies, bishops, princes, and kings, but masters of huge industries turning out commodities by the ton and the million could thrive in no such limited area of demand. Markets for mass production simply could not be found unless the masses themselves rose above the historic margin of subsistence and were able to buy by the ton and the million. Only when the standard of life for the multitude is constantly rising and buying capacity is expanding can widening outlets be found for the goods which pour in swelling streams from the vast industries made possible by science and machinery. If the American bourgeois were as indifferent, on moral grounds, to the lot of the masses as the French nobility of the eighteenth century to the plight of their laborious peasants, still their enterprises could not develop without a continuous enlargement of the popular market—without a steady growth in the capacity of the masses to buy and enjoy goods once confined to the classes . . .

If critics of progress fail to grasp its cosmic nature, friends of the idea often make it appear petty and ridiculous by the undiscriminating zeal with which they espouse it. As in the case of every other fruitful concept, a lunatic fringe is associated with the idea. To these short-sighted spectators at the great show, all movement is progress, means are ends, and the worth of a personality is to be measured by the number of motor-cars, telephones, radios, and bathtubs he possesses. The idea of progress thus becomes purely numerical. J. P. Morgan has more things than Dante; therefore he is superior. Jim Fiske had more diamond rings than Francis of Assisi; accordingly, his rating in civilization must be higher. Zenith has more miles of paved streets than Athens, a single apartment house in New York will hold the entire population of that ancient city; evidently America transcends in achievement the best of the Greeks. Thus a noble concept of humanity is made both absurd and contemptible, obnoxious in the house of its friends, and a shining target for abuse at the hands of its opponents.

Yet when the critics and scoffers, writing under soft lamps or lecturing for fees to well-fed audiences, in comfortable rooms electrically lighted, venture to speak of an alternative, they can only offer a return to agriculture and handicrafts. Overlooking the fact that they can themselves go at any time to any one of a thousand waste places awaiting the plow or the hoe, they prefer to advise others to incur the risk. When asked for a bill of particulars, they become hazy and vague. Are we merely to surrender the tractor and return to the steel plow? Why not to the wooden plow? Or better still, to the forked stick hardened by fire? Each advance on the most primitive instrument is a gain in efficiency, a transfer of labor from man to a tool. In the process of retreat are surgery and dentistry to go into the discard? Sanitation, antiseptics, and anesthetics? Each of these gains has marked a step in progress or rather a long series of steps, and each art steadily advances in our own time as masters of the test tube and microscope penetrate deeper and deeper into the mysteries of nature. Fundamentally the machine differs from the tool in degree, not in kind, and the chemist works in materials no less than did the most primitive woman herbalist. His knowledge is wider, his skill is greater, but his ends may well be fundamentally the same—the relief of human suffering. Where then is the line to be drawn? To what point in the long upward progress of mankind is the return to be made? To ask these questions is to answer them. The severest critic of progress is forced to admit, when cornered, that the problem is not one of retreat, but of ends and methods, of choices and uses.

If in the hands of its superficial champions the idea of progress seems to emphasize means rather than ends, an examination into the history and nature of the concept shows that this notion is without basis. Although selfish men have seized upon the instrumentalities of progress and have left in the train of their exploits hideous industrial cities, slums, poverty, and misery, that upshot is no more to be attributed to the idea itself than the cruelties of the Inquisition to the teachings of Jesus. An inquiry into the writings of those who originated and developed the theory of progress shows at the center of their thought the concept of the good life as the end of progressive endeavor, the genius which is to preside over the searches and labors of explorers and experimenters. The good life for the multitude, not for a superior minority living in a land of illusion on the sweat of the "ignoble"—this is the kernel germinating in the heart of the concept of progress. To see life whole and to see it steadily, to sound its deeps, to illuminate its possibilities, and to make the noblest and wisest use of material resources in realizing its purposes, this is the sum total of the idea of progress—a grand end, conceived in the light of universality, appealing to a mankind seeking high destiny and striving for mastery over the instrumentalities to be employed by the way. Anything less than this is a caricature of the idea.

Wrongly identified with capitalism, communism, or particular systems of economy, though standing at the very threshold of the great analysis and inquest, the idea of progress nevertheless clearly reveals the method by which ends are to be attained. Its method is that of science and technology—rationality, in short. And that method implies many things. It implies an open-eyed and open-minded attitude toward tasks in hand and problems to be solved. Working with concrete materials under positive law, technology is as indifferent to the emotional idiosyncrasies of individuals and classes as the elements themselves. Universal in its reach, as transcendent as the gods, it cannot be monopolized by any nation, period, class, government, or race. Its catholicity surpasses that of all religions. Essentially objective in its manipulations, dealing with materials, quantities, and known laws, technology is leveling and democratic in its effects; it is not a closed cult handed down by a few masters to a few students in cloistered universities. Rational in nature, corresponding to the mathematics of physical things and forces, this method is necessarily planful. It cannot begin anything without a goal, project, or purpose. To proceed at all it must stake out a field of work, a problem to be solved, and then it must proceed according to plan, on the assumption of predictable results, to predetermined ends. Inexorably, therefore, it cuts across the wild welter of unreasoned actions, irrelevant sentiments, and emotional starts and fits which have so long characterized human life in historic politics, industry, agriculture, and esthetics. Rational and playful, working in the unity of all things, this method is centripetal, drawing all arts, economies, and sciences inward toward the unity of the world—with implications so vast, so in harmony with mankind's noblest dreams, that the imagination is staggered by them.

Since the rationality of progress imposes limitations on inner impulses and cuts across external arrangements, it inevitably involves all departments of human activity—pure science, invention, industry, transportation, agriculture, government, finance, medicine, social adjustments, the work of women, education, arts, and letters. As the first carved gates of ancient Egypt celebrated the purpose of the ruling monarch, so the latest skyscraper in New York reflects the functions of its inhabitants. All branches of civilization mirror the dominant idea. If the escape of negation be sought, it will be found blocked at the exit. All arts, sciences, and crafts are drawn into the movement of regnant thought and practice. And when the thought of the thinker, the dream of the artist, and the aspiration of the practitioner draw together under a common principle of unification, the light and heat required for heroic endeavor are generated, giving to each the power of the whole, suffusing all with a sense of elevation and movement, supplying energy to the weak, and providing for the strong and willful who make history that social dynamic without which even Napoleon himself might have been a Corsican lawyer or Genoese scrivener.

"The Assault on Integrity"
By Alan Greenspan
1976

The Industrial Revolution's sweeping changes in industrial organization led to incredible concentrations of economic power and wealth never before seen. Many critics of the system called for government regulation to curb the abuses they saw happening as a result of this monopolization of economic production.

Some of the legislation that resulted called for reforms, such as the Food and Drug Act, which created the Federal Food and Drug Administration, and the Sherman Antitrust Act, whose most recent application was in the antitrust case against Microsoft during the late 1990s. These bills, and the agencies and departments they created, granted sweeping new powers to the federal government to regulate businesses in an attempt to prevent them from abusing the public trust. In turn they required an expansion of the federal bureaucracy, which required new sources of revenue, in the form of higher taxes, in order to fund them.

This last development became a rallying cry for those who believed that these taxes stifled the ability of the private sector to grow. They felt that the marketplace's own internal dynamics would prevent abuses of consumers. The following piece was written in the 1970s, by Alan Greenspan, the chairman of the Federal Reserve since 1987. Here Greenspan discusses the need to protect the consumer from the Industrial Revolution's most deplorable legacy—greed.

Protection of the consumer against "dishonest and unscrupulous business practices" has become a cardinal ingredient of welfare statism. Left to their own devices, it is alleged, businessmen would attempt to sell unsafe food and drugs, fraudulent securities, and shoddy buildings. Thus, it is argued, the Pure Food and Drug Administration, the Securities and Exchange Commission, and the numerous building regulatory agencies are indispensable if the consumer is to be protected from the "greed" of the businessman.

But it is precisely the "greed" of the businessman or, more appropriately, his profit-seeking, which is the unexcelled protector of the consumer.

What collectivists refuse to recognize is that it is in the self-interest of every businessman to have a reputation for honest dealings and a quality product. Since the market value of a going business is measured by its money-making potential, reputation or "good will" is as much an asset as its physical plant and equipment. For many a drug company, the value of its reputation, as reflected in the salability of its brand name, is often its major asset. The loss of reputation through the sale of a shoddy or dangerous product would sharply reduce the market value of the drug company, though its physical resources would remain intact. The market value of a brokerage firm is even more closely tied to its good-will assets. Securities worth hundreds of millions of dollars are traded every day over the telephone. The slightest doubt as to the trustworthiness of a broker's word or commitment would put him out of business overnight.

Reputation, in an unregulated economy, is thus a major competitive tool. Builders who have acquired a reputation for top quality construction take the market away from their less scrupulous or less conscientious competitors. The most reputable securities dealers get the bulk of the commission business. Drug manufacturers and food processors vie with one another to make their brand names synonymous with fine quality.

Physicians have to be just as scrupulous in judging the quality of the drugs they prescribe. They, too, are in business and compete for trustworthiness. Even the corner grocer is involved: he cannot afford to sell unhealthy foods if he wants to make money. In fact, in one way or another, every producer and distributor of goods or services is caught up in competition for reputation.

It requires years of consistently excellent performance to acquire a reputation and to establish it as a financial asset. Thereafter, a still greater effort is required to maintain it: a company cannot afford to risk its years of investment by letting down its standards of quality for one moment or one inferior product; nor would it be tempted by any potential "quick killing." Newcomers entering the field cannot compete immediately with the established, reputable companies, and have to spend years working on a more modest scale in order to earn an equal reputation. Thus the incentive to scrupulous performance operates on all levels of a given field of product. It is a built-in safeguard of a free enterprise system and only real protection of consumers against business dishonesty.

Government regulation is not an alternative means of protecting the consumer. It does not build quality into goods, or accuracy into information. Its sole "contribution" is to substitute force and fear for incentive as the "protector" of the consumer. The euphemisms of government press releases to the contrary notwithstanding, the basis of regulation is armed force. At the bottom of the endless pile of paper work which characterizes all regulation lies a gun. What are the results?

To paraphrase Gresham's Law: bad "protection" drives out good. The attempt to protect the consumer by force undercuts the protection he gets from incentive. First, it undercuts the value of reputation by placing the reputable company on the same basis as the unknown, the newcomer, or the fly-by-nighter. It declares, in effect, that all are equally suspect and that years of evidence to the contrary do not free a man from that suspicion. Second, it grants an automatic (though, in fact, unachievable) guarantee of safety to the products of any company that complies with its arbitrarily set minimum standards. The value of a reputation rested on the fact that it was necessary for the consumers to exercise judgment in the choice of the goods and services they purchased. The government's "guarantee" undermines this necessity; it declares to the consumers, in effect, that no choice or judgment is required—and that a company's record, its years of achievement, is irrelevant.

The minimum standards, which are the basis of regulation, gradually tend to become the maximums as well. If the building codes set minimum standards of construction, a builder does not get very much competitive advantage by exceeding those standards and, accordingly, he tends to meet only the minimums. If minimum specifications are set for vitamins, there is little profit in producing something of above-average quality. Gradually, even the attempt to maintain minimum standards becomes impossible, since the draining of incentives to improve quality ultimately undermines even the minimums.

The guiding purpose of the government regulator is to prevent rather than to create something. He gets no credit if a new miraculous drug is discovered by drug company scientists; he does if he bans thalidomide. Such emphasis on the negative sets the framework under which even the most conscientious regulator must operate. The result is a growing body of restrictive legislation on drug experimentation, testing, and distribution. As in all research, it is impossible to add restrictions to the development of new drugs without simultaneously cutting off the secondary rewards of such research—the improvement of existing drugs. Quality improvement and innovation are inseparable.

Building codes are supposed to protect the public. But by being forced to adhere to standards of construction long after they have been surpassed by the technological discoveries, builders divert their efforts to maintaining the old rather than adopting new and safer techniques of construction.

Regulation—which is based on force and fear—undermines the moral base of business dealings. It becomes cheaper to bribe a building inspector than to meet his standards of construction. A fly-by-night securities operator can quickly meet all the S.E.C. requirements, gain the inference of respectability, and proceed to fleece the public. In an unregulated economy, the operator would have had to spend a number of years in reputable dealings before he could earn a position of trust sufficient to induce a number of investors to place funds with him.

Protection of the consumer by regulation is thus illusory. Rather than isolating the consumer from the dishonest businessman, it is gradually destroying the only reliable protection the consumer has: competition for reputation.

While the consumer is thus endangered, the major victim of "protective" regulation is the producer: the businessman. Regulation which acts to destroy the competition of businessmen for reputation undermines the market value of the good will which businessmen have built up over the years. It is an act of expropriation of wealth created by integrity. Since the value of a business—its wealth—rests on its ability to make money, the acts of a government seizing a company's plant devaluing its reputation are in the same category: both are acts of expropriation.

Moreover, "protective" legislation falls in the category of preventive law. Businessmen are being subjected to governmental coercion *prior* to the commission of any crime. In a free economy, the government may step in only when a fraud has been perpetrated, or a demonstrable damage has been done to a consumer; in such cases the only protection required is that of criminal law.

Government regulations do not eliminate potentially dishonest individuals, but merely make their activities harder to detect or easier to hush up. Furthermore, the possibility of individual dishonesty applies to government employees fully as much as to any other group of men. There is nothing to guarantee the superior judgment, knowledge, and integrity of an inspector or a bureaucrat—and the deadly consequences of entrusting him with arbitrary power are obvious.

The hallmark of collectivists is their deep-rooted distrust of freedom and of the free-market processes; but it is their advocacy of so-called "consumer protection" that exposes the nature of their basic premises with particular clarity. By preferring force and fear to incentive and reward as a means of human motivation, they confess their view of man as a mindless brute functioning on the range of the moment, whose actual self-interest lies in "flying-by-night" and making "quick kills." They confess their ignorance of the role of intelligence in the production process, of the wide intellectual context and long-range vision required to maintain a modern industry. They confess their inability to grasp the crucial importance of the moral values which are the motive power of capitalism. Capitalism is based on self-interest and self-esteem; it holds integrity and trustworthiness as cardinal virtues and makes them pay off in the marketplace, thus demanding that men survive by means of virtues, not of vices. It is this superlatively moral system that the welfare statistics propose to improve upon by means of preventive law, snooping bureaucrats, and the chronic goad of fear.

TIMELINE

1712 — In England, Thomas Newcomen invents a workable steam engine.

1775 — James Watt invents a more efficient and practical steam engine than the Newcomen engine. This becomes the template for further innovations in steam power.

1793 — Eli Whitney invents the cotton gin. This makes processing picked cotton much more efficient, but it also makes slaves indispensable to the Southern economy in America. Whitney also pioneers the idea of mass-produced interchangeable parts in manufacturing.

1811–1815 — Luddites (an organization of English hand-craftsmen) riot to protest the factories that they fear will cost them their jobs. This is one of the first organized attempts by workers to control the pace and scope of industrialization.

1837 — Samuel F. B. Morse invents the telegraph and Morse code.

1848 — Karl Marx's *Communist Manifesto,* which indicts the capitalist system brought into being by the Industrial Revolution, is published.

1855 — Henry Bessemer patents his new steel-making process, which becomes the basis for the modern steel industry.

1876 — Alexander Graham Bell invents the telephone.

1879 — Thomas Edison invents the incandescent light, making electric lighting practical and affordable.

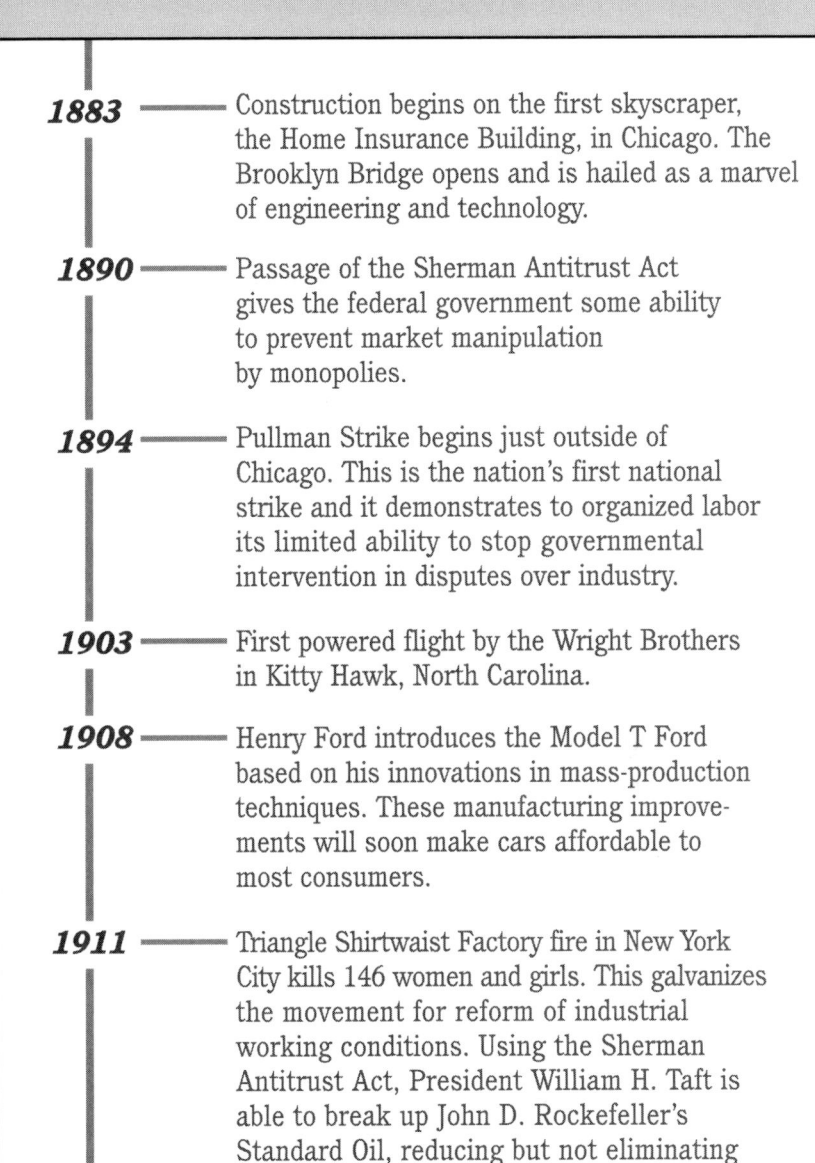

1883 — Construction begins on the first skyscraper, the Home Insurance Building, in Chicago. The Brooklyn Bridge opens and is hailed as a marvel of engineering and technology.

1890 — Passage of the Sherman Antitrust Act gives the federal government some ability to prevent market manipulation by monopolies.

1894 — Pullman Strike begins just outside of Chicago. This is the nation's first national strike and it demonstrates to organized labor its limited ability to stop governmental intervention in disputes over industry.

1903 — First powered flight by the Wright Brothers in Kitty Hawk, North Carolina.

1908 — Henry Ford introduces the Model T Ford based on his innovations in mass-production techniques. These manufacturing improvements will soon make cars affordable to most consumers.

1911 — Triangle Shirtwaist Factory fire in New York City kills 146 women and girls. This galvanizes the movement for reform of industrial working conditions. Using the Sherman Antitrust Act, President William H. Taft is able to break up John D. Rockefeller's Standard Oil, reducing but not eliminating the power that this huge conglomerate has on America's economic life.

For More Information

Web Sites

Due to the changing nature of Internet links, the Rosen Publishing Group, Inc., has developed an online list of Web sites related to the subject of this book. This site is updated regularly. Please use this link to access the list:

http://www.rosenlinks.com/canf/inre

For Further Reading

Bernhardt, Debra E. *Ordinary People, Extraordinary Lives: A Pictorial History of Working People in New York City*. New York: New York University Press, 2000.

Brinkley, Douglas. *Wheels for the World: Henry Ford, His Company, and a Century of Progress, 1903–2003*. New York: Viking, 2003.

Chernow, Ron. *Titan: The Life of John D. Rockefeller*. New York: Random House, 1998.

Hindle, Brooke, and Steven Lubar. *Engines of Change: The American Industrial Revolution, 1790-1860*. Washington, D.C.: Smithsonian Institution Press, 1986.

Hobsbawm, Eric. *Industry and Empire: The Birth of the Industrial Revolution*. New York: New Press, 1999.

Reid, B. H., and J. Keegan. *The American Civil War and the Wars of the Industrial Revolution*. London: Cassell, 1999.

Stearns, Peter N. *The Industrial Revolution in World History*. New York: Westview Press, 1993.

Stearns, P. N., J. H. Hinshaw, et al. *The ABC-CLIO World History Companion to the Industrial Revolution*. Santa Barbara, CA: ABC-CLIO, 1996.

Young, Marguerite. *Harp Song for a Radical: The Life and Times of Eugene Victor*. New York: Alfred A. Knopf, 1999.

Historical Fiction

Alger, Horatio. *Ragged Dick*. New York: Penguin Books, 1984.

Lewis, Sinclair. *Babbitt*. New York: Penguin Books, 1996.

Sinclair, Upton. *The Jungle*. New York: Penguin Books, 1986.

ANNOTATED BIBLIOGRAPHY

"Aguinaldo's Case Against the United States." *The North American Review*, University of Northern Iowa Publishers, Vol. 169, Issue 514, September 1899.

A rebuttal of the United States' policy in the Philippines after the Spanish-American War written by an anonymous author, perhaps even by the leader of the Filipino opposition, Emilio Aguinaldo, himself.

Baker, Ray Stannard. "The Right to Work." *McClure's*, Vol. XX, No. 3, January 1903.

Written by one of the founders of the muckraking reportorial style, this in-depth account of violence against non-union workers by striking unionized coal workers is a master example of the style.

Beard, Charles A., ed. *A Century of Progress*. New York: Harper and Brothers Publishers, 1933.

A leading scholar of American history in the early twentieth century, Beard analyzes the concept of progress and how it has shaped the development of American culture and society in this compilation of essays.

Byrn, Edward W. "The Progress of Invention During the Past Fifty Years," *Scientific American*, July 25, 1896.

A typical piece of late-nineteenth-century journalism praising industrialization without anticipating its consequences.

"Child Labor Accounts." Farmington Hills, MI: The Gale Research Group, 1998.

Testimony taken in order to document the horrible abuse

that children endured while working in England's factories.

Crane, Stephen. Edited by Fredson Bowers. *Reports of the War*. Charlottesville, VA: The University Press of Virginia, 1971.

At the turn of the twentieth century, the author of *The Red Badge of Courage* went into various war zones, providing sympathetic coverage of the troops and their struggles, for New York's newspapers .

"The Delirium of Dress." *The Living Age*. Seventh series, Volume V. Boston: The Living Age Company, October, November, December 1899.

An unsigned humorous and sarcastic look at how fashion has come to dominate the thinking of women of all social classes.

Dickens, Charles. "A Nightly Scene in London." *Harper's Magazine*, Vol. 12, Issue 71, April 1856.

England's foremost author and critic of the societal havoc caused by the Industrial Revolution documents his encounter with poverty-stricken women on London's streets.

Edison, Thomas. "The Success of the Electric Light." *The North American Review*, Vol. 131, Issue 287, October 1880.

Thomas Edison was the country's most prolific inventor, bringing the public such devices as the phonograph, movie camera, and, of course, incandescent electric lights. Edison details the struggles he overcame to perfect this last accomplishment.

Filene, Edward A. "Mass Production Makes a Better World." *Atlantic Monthly*, May 1929.

As a leader in mass merchandising, Edward Filene uses his

experience to explain and justify all the benefits that the mass production factory system has brought to consumers.

Flower, Elliott. "Gary, the Magic City." *Putnam's Magazine*, Vol. 5, No. 6, 1909.

This is a stirring report of the creation of the city of Gary, Indiana, as a model city for industrial concerns and workers.

Ford, Henry T. "Where High Wages Begin." Farmington Hills, MI: The Gale Research Group, 1998. Copyright © 1975, Gale Group. Reprinted with permission of the Gale Group.

Henry Ford's defense of his own policy to pay his workers a sufficient wage includes the proposition that labor and capital must work together for both to succeed.

Greenspan, Alan. Edited by Ayn Rand. "The Assault on Integrity." *Capitalism: The Unknown Ideal*. New York: New American Library, 1976.

In this strongly worded essay on the value of free and open markets, Greenspan describes the philosophy that would later play a strong role in his economic policies as chairman of the Federal Reserve Board.

Marx, Karl, and Friedrich Engels. *The Communist Manifesto*. New York: Penguin Putnam, 1998.

A deep analytical critique of the ills and inequalities caused by the capitalist economic system, as well as the authors' proposed revolutionary solutions.

McKinley, William. Address at Minneapolis. October 12, 1899.

Retrieved from Lexis Nexis June 2003. President McKinley defends his Philippines policies in a speech given before business leaders and supporters.

Muir, John. "The American Forests." *Atlantic Monthly*, Vol. LXXX, August 1897. America's "father" of the environmental movement passionately advocates for the defense of forests, woods, and wildlands as a national treasure.

Debs, Eugene V. "A Declaration of Principles." Stead, W. T. *Chicago To-Day: The Labor War in America*. New York: Arno Press & The New York Times, 1969. Copyright © 1969 by New York Times Co. Reprinted with permission. A compilation of various points of view about the causes, happenings, and consequences of the 1894 Chicago Pullman Strike.

Sumner, William. *Essays of William Sumner*. New Haven, CT: Yale University Press, 1934. Copyright © 1934 by Yale University Press. Reprinted with Permission. In this collection of essays, the leading sociologist of his generation Sumner turns his keen scholar's eye on questions of societal organization and economic equality.

Twain, Mark. "A Telephonic Conversation." *The Atlantic Monthly*, Vol. 45, Issue 267, January 1880. The foremost American humorist tackles the new challenges to etiquette that technological changes bring with them.

Wells, H. G. *The Outline of History*. New York: Garden City Books, 1949. H. G. Wells turns his prophetic gifts as a writer to compose an in-depth history of the world, including the impact of science and technology in this two-volume text.

Wright, C. D. "Science, Invention, Industry." *Current Literature* (1888–1912). Vol. VIII, Issue 3, November 1891.

A brief overview of the various inventions and technologies that helped to create and transform the American industrial system prior to 1900.

INDEX

A
Address at Minneapolis by William McKinley, 120–126
Aguinaldo, Emilio, 120, 126–127
American Railway Union, 71, 77
Arkwright, Richard, 6

B
Baker, Ray Stannard, article excerpt on labor disputes, 60–65
Beard, Charles A., 148–149
  essay on industrial progress, 149–157
Benevolent Assimilation Proclamation, 127
Brindley, James, 5
Byrn, Edward W., essay on the progress of invention, 50–58

C
Carnegie, Andrew, 86, 119–120
child labor, 65–66
  testimonial excerpts, 66–70
Cleveland, President Grover, 71
coal mining, 5, 11, 14
communism, 17, 26
Communist Manifesto, The, 16
  excerpt, 17–25
Crane, Stephen, 136
  dispatch excerpt, 137–140
Crompton, Samuel, 5
Curtiss, Glenn H., 14

D
Debs, Eugene V., 71–72
"A Declaration of Principles," 72–77
department stores, creation of, 141–142
Dewey, Admiral George, 127, 135
Dickens, Charles, 102
  article on urban life, 102–109

E
Edison, Thomas A., 43–44, 53, 54, 55
  essay on electric light, 44–49
electric light, 13, 14, 36, 43–44, 52, 53
  essay by Thomas A. Edison, 44–49
Engels, Friedrich, 16

F
Factory Act, 65
Fair Labor Standards Act, 65–66
Faraday, Michael, 12
fashion and industrialization, article on, 93–101
Filene, Edward A., 142
  essay on mass production, 142–148
Flower, Elliott, essay on Gary, Indiana, 86–92
flying shuttle, 5
Food and Drug Act, 157
Ford, Henry, 77–78
  essay on wages, 78–84
forests, American, essay by John Muir, 110–118
free trade, 26–27
  essay by William Graham Sumner, 27–32

173

G

Galvani, Luigi, 12
Gary, Elbert, 86
Gary, Indiana, 86
   essay by Elliott Flower, 86–92
Great Britain, industrial developments in, 4–6
Greenspan, Alan, 158
   essay on protecting consumers from greed, 158–163
guild system, 4

H

Hargreaves, James, 5
Hobsbawm, Eric, 4

I

immigrants/immigration, 7–8, 65
industrial progress/progress of invention
   essay by C. D. Wright, 33–37
   essay by Charles A. Beard, 149–157
   essay by Edward W. Byrn, 50–58

J

James, William, 120

K

Kay, John, 5

L

labor unions/labor disputes, 59–60, 77
   article excerpt by Ray Stannard Baker, 60–65

"A Declaration of Principles" by Eugene V. Debs, 72–77
laissez-faire capitalism, explanation of, 26
Langley, Samuel P., 14
Lenin, Vladimir, 17

M

Marx, Karl, 16–17, 26
   excerpt from *The Communist Manifesto*, 17–25
mass production, essay by Edward A. Filene, 142–148
McKinley, William, 119, 127
   Address at Minneapolis, 120–126
Morgan, J. P., 86, 153
Muir, John, 109–110
   essay on American forests, 110–118
mule, 5, 34

N

Nasmyth, James, 13
Newcomen steam engine, 5

O

Outline of History, The, by H. G. Wells, excerpt from, 10–16

P

Philippines, 119–120, 126–127
   Address at Minneapolis by William McKinley, 120–126
   anonymous essay on independence, 127–135
Pullman, George, 71, 85
Pullman, Illinois, 85, 86

INDEX

Pullman Strike of 1894, 71–72

R
Red Badge of Courage, The, 136
Russian Revolution, 17

S
Schwab, Charles, 86
Sherman Antitrust Act, 157
Sierra Club, 110
Slater, Samuel, 6
Smith, Adam, 26
Soviet Union, 17
Spanish-American War, 119, 127, 136
    dispatch excerpt by Stephen Crane, 137–140
steam power/steam engines, 5, 6, 11, 12, 14, 47, 52
Stephenson, George, 6
Sumner, William Graham, 26
    essay on free trade, 27–32

T
telegraph, 12, 36, 43, 47, 52, 53, 54

Trevithick, Richard, 11
Twain, Mark, 38, 119–120
    "A Telephonic Conversation," 38–43

U
United States Steel Corporation, 86, 88
urban life, article by Charles Dickens, 102–109

V
Volta, Alessandro, 12

W
wages, essay by Henry T. Ford, 78–84
Watt, James, 5, 11, 14
Wells, H. G., 9–10
    excerpt from *The Outline of History*, 10–16
Westinghouse, George, 44
Wright, C. D., essay on industrial progress, 33–37

About the Editor

Josh Sakolsky is a freelance writer and graduate student at Columbia University's Teachers College pursuing studies in history and education. He lives in New Jersey with his wife, Stacy, and two fuzzy kids—Thumper (a rabbit) and Hydro (a German shepherd).

Photo Credits

Cover © Hulton/Archive/Getty Images, Inc.

Designer: Thomas Forget; Series Editor: Charles Hofer